DATE DUE

Dr. Miriam Stoppard

DK

YOUR NEW BABY

HEALTHCARE

DORLING KINDERSLEY
London • New York • Sydney • Moscow

A DORLING KINDERSLEY BOOK

DESIGN AND EDITORIAL   Mason Linklater

SENIOR MANAGING
ART EDITOR   Lynne Brown
MANAGING EDITOR   Jemima Dunne

SENIOR ART EDITOR   Karen Ward
SENIOR EDITOR   Penny Warren

PRODUCTION   Antony Heller

First published in Great Britain in 1998 by
Dorling Kindersley Limited, 9 Henrietta Street,
Covent Garden, London WC2E 8PS

Visit us on the World Wide Web at
http://www.dk.com

A CIP catalogue record for this book is available
from the British Library

ISBN 0-7513-0552-9

Reproduced by Colourscan, Singapore
and IGS, Radstock, Avon
Printed in Hong Kong by
Wing King Tong

CONTENTS

INTRODUCTION

Whether you're a mother expecting your first baby, or have just given birth, or are an expectant or new father, you may be feeling apprehensive about your new role. Your delight at the prospect of having a baby may be mixed with anxiety about whether you'll be a good parent and can cope with bringing up a child. On top of this, you'll feel concerned for the happiness of your child if you mess things up. Don't worry: while parenting is one of the most responsible and challenging of all jobs, it's also one of the most rewarding.

THE NEWBORN BABY

You've just experienced the creation of new life. Your baby is probably smaller than you imagined and he may seem very vulnerable. You may feel overwhelmed by joy, but you'll also be anxious to know whether your baby is all right, and whether the sounds and movements he makes are normal. Your doctor or midwife will do a few simple tests right after delivery, and the next day, to check that your baby is healthy. This will reassure you, and you'll probably be surprised at just how much your baby can do.

It's important for father and baby to bond, too. While mothers usually take most responsibility for a newborn's care, the father should be encouraged to take an equal role. From the start, your baby's father should learn how to hold and care for your newborn. This way, your baby will very soon come to associate his father's specific smell and touch, and the sound of his voice, with comfort and reassurance.

LOVING TOUCH

All children benefit from close physical contact. You'll find that you instinctively hold your baby close, look into his eyes and talk soothingly to him. He's more robust than you might think and knowing this may help you to feel at ease when you handle him. Feeding, bathing, changing and dressing will go more smoothly if you can hold him confidently.

All babies cry quite a lot; it's their only way of letting you know what they need. Within a few weeks, you'll learn to distinguish between the different cries that show your baby is hungry, niggling because he's bored, wants to be put down to sleep or just wants a cuddle. Sometimes he'll cry for no obvious reason, but there are many remedies you can try to soothe and console him. Always be sensitive and alert to your baby's needs and respond quite quickly to his cry. If you don't respond, he'll feel just as you would if you were ignored in a conversation.

FEEDING AND NUTRITION

Your newborn baby depends on you to meet all his nutritional needs. Feeding takes up a great deal of time, so it's essential to choose a method that suits you both. Breast milk is the perfect food. It contains all the nutrients in just the right amounts your baby needs. From your point of view, breastfeeding is also very convenient: there's no equipment to buy or sterilize and no formula to make up. If you can't breastfeed or choose not to, your baby will still thrive on a good bottlefed diet, and one of the benefits of bottlefeeding is that your partner can be equally involved with feeding your baby.

EVERYDAY CARE

Keeping your baby strong and healthy means not just giving him a good diet but also looking after his physical comfort and hygiene each day. Many new parents worry about handling a very small baby in the baby bath, but you'll soon get used to bathtime and look forward to it as an opportunity to have fun and play with your baby. Instead of feeling anxious, set aside half an hour, have everything around you, try to relax and you'll enjoy the experience.

Your newborn baby may need up to ten nappy changes a day and you'll hardly believe there was once a time when you didn't know how to change a nappy! You can opt for disposable or fabric nappies, and will want to know the pros and cons of using either kind. Preventing nappy rash also means practising good nappy hygiene and you'll minimize the possibility of nappy rash if you follow a few commonsense guidelines (continued p. 8).

With first clothes for your baby, look for cosy, comfortable garments in soft, natural fabrics that you can put on and take off him with the minimum of fuss. Dressing your baby will get easier with practice, so just be gentle and patient until you both get the hang of it.

SLEEPING

Unless your newborn is hungry, cold or uncomfortable in some other way, he'll spend most of the time between feeds asleep. It's important to consider what he'll sleep in and his sleeping environment, since research has shown that babies who get too hot are at a greater risk of cot death. Try to encourage your baby to sleep at night by tiring him out in the day with plenty of stimulation. If he frequently wakes you during the night, you'll find it difficult to cope.

GOING OUT AND ABOUT

Being organized and confident makes outings with your baby a great joy and the sooner you start after bringing him home the better. When choosing equipment to carry or transport your baby, safety and portability should be your main considerations. It's worth spending time planning any trip so that you'll know where you can stop to change and feed your baby without inconvenience. For longer trips by car, preparation and attention to safety are paramount.

THE REWARDS OF PARENTING

A rule I've learned about parenting is that whatever you put in you'll get back five hundred times over. The sacrifices you make when your baby is very young will be replaced by more and more pleasures. One of the greatest is to watch your baby develop and change from being dependent and demanding into a charming and thoughtful companion, an entertaining friend and a good pal.

THE NEWBORN BABY

You're likely to feel pride, wonder and exhilaration, mixed
with exhaustion, on the birth of your baby. You may
feel deeply attached to her straight away, or bonding
may take a little longer. You'll almost certainly be surprised
at your baby's appearance – her oddly shaped head,
wrinkled face and tiny hands and feet – and your first
question will be "Is she all right?".

From the moment of birth, your baby will exhibit
reflexes and behaviour that help her survive. In such
things as her sleeping patterns and crying bouts, you'll be
able to discern the beginnings of a unique personality.

Most mothers find they establish a tangible bond with their newborn babies within the first 72 hours, but a "bond" doesn't necessarily mean instantaneous and ecstatic love at first sight.

Attending to the physical needs of your newborn baby is so exhausting that it's easy to forget your baby also has an active emotional life. In the long term, the most serious damage to a baby's health may stem from inadequate love and attention; so in the next few weeks and months, heap as much of both upon your baby as you can.

Mother love is partially hormonal, so if you don't feel it immediately it's not your fault. Mother love usually comes in with the milk, 72 hours after the birth of your child, though it may come in later and it may grow quite gradually. One of the hormones that stimulates lactation is also responsible for mother love, in part.

Some mothers are shocked to find that they lack maternal feelings when they first hold their babies. This may be due to a variety of factors, such as complications with the delivery, unrealistic expectations of childbirth, sheer exhaustion, fluctuating hormone levels, and even the mother's own experience in early childhood. Maternal "indifference" can last from an hour to a week, but rarely much longer.

YOUR NEW BABY

Whatever you had expected – bigger, smaller, quieter, less slippery – your baby will be a surprise and delight to you. Experienced parents discern a personality at birth but first-time parents may think their newborns are oblivious to the world about them. Babies, however, rapidly build up a vocabulary of sensory experiences right from the moment of birth. When awake, your baby will be alert and listening. She can respond when spoken to, recognizes you by smell, and has an intent gaze. At birth she can recognize a human face, and she will move her head in response to noise. She is born wanting to talk and will "converse" with you if you talk animatedly, holding your head about 20–25 centimetres (8–10 inches) from her face; at this distance, she will be able to see you clearly. She will react to your smile in several ways: by moving her mouth, nodding, protruding her tongue, or jerking her whole body.

HANDLING YOUR BABY

The need for physical contact throughout childhood is well documented, and this is especially true of the first weeks of life. The majority of newborn babies spend much of their time asleep, so it is important that you're there to hold, mother, and respond to your baby when she's awake. If your baby is in an incubator, ask to be able to stroke her and change her nappy, at least. One young mother I met recently, whose ten-day-old baby had been in an incubator for the first 48 hours, was too terrified to pick him up because she thought he might "break". Babies are physically stronger than you might think.

YOUR BABY'S BREATHING

After an initial outburst of crying, you may not be able to hear anything more from your baby because it can be difficult to hear a newborn's light breathing. In some cases a baby may even stop breathing entirely for a few seconds, but this isn't abnormal or even cause for concern. All babies make strange noises when they breathe – usually a noisy, snuffling sound – and their breathing is often irregular.

Your baby's lungs are still weak, which means that her breathing is naturally much shallower and more rapid than yours or mine. This is nothing to worry about, as her lungs will gradually get stronger each day.

SUCKLING

For the first three days after your baby's birth, your breasts produce not milk, but colostrum, a thin, yellow fluid that contains water, protein, sugar, vitamins, minerals, and antibodies that give protection against infectious diseases. During her first 72 hours of life, colostrum helps protect your baby against infections. To stimulate your breasts to produce milk, you need to feed her frequently; the sucking action of the baby stimulates hormones that, in turn, stimulate milk production. Even if you do not intend to breastfeed, it is a good idea to suckle your baby as soon as she is born, because the colostrum will be beneficial to her, and the act of suckling will help you bond with your baby.

As soon as your baby is born you can put her to your breast. Her natural sucking reflex and the sucking action will encourage the production of the hormone oxytocin. Oxytocin makes the uterus contract and expel the placenta. Touch your baby's cheek on the side nearest your nipple to stimulate her rooting reflex (see p. 38). Her lips should be on the breast tissue, with the whole of the nipple in her mouth.

INVOLVING YOUR PARTNER

Because the experience of childbirth is so focused on the mother it is common for the father to feel neglected or excluded. It is important for father and baby to bond, too; touch, smell, and sound are good ways to do this. Soon after his baby is born, her father should hold her against his skin; this way his baby will come into contact with his specific smell and over a period of weeks she will learn to associate this with comfort and reassurance. The father should also speak to his child as she will quickly become familiar with his voice. In fact, if he talks to the baby while she is in the uterus, she will recognize her father's voice when she is born.

It is common for the mother to take prime responsibility for a newborn's care, but the father should be encouraged to take an equal role. He should learn how to hold his baby and should build up a tactile relationship with her. Make sure he becomes involved with day-to-day routines such as bathing and nappy changing. Even if the baby is breastfed, he can learn to bottlefeed her by using expressed breastmilk from the mother. Both parents should cuddle the baby when she and they are both naked, so that she can feel and smell your skin and hear both your hearts beating.

YOUR BABY'S FIRST BREATH

Don't be alarmed if your newborn cries vigorously – this is exactly the sound you want to hear.

Inside the uterus, your baby's lungs are redundant. She gets all the oxygen she needs from the placenta, so the lungs are temporarily collapsed.

The very first time your baby takes a breath, the lungs expand, and the increased pressure in them shuts a valve just beyond the heart, so that the blood that used to pass to the placenta for oxygenation now goes directly to the lungs. These two crucial actions make her an independent being, able to survive without you, and they happen in an instant.

Nothing should interfere with your baby's ability to take her first breath. That's why doctors and midwives clear air passages immediately and if the first breath is delayed, they will resuscitate the baby.

SPOTS AND RASHES

Most newborns have harmless skin irritations, such as spots and rashes, in the first few days. They generally clear up when the skin begins to stabilize, at around about three weeks old.

Milia These small white spots are seen mainly on the bridge of the nose, but also elsewhere on the face. They're the result of a temporary blockage of the sebaceous glands, which secrete sebum to lubricate the skin. Never squeeze them: they will disappear of their own accord within a few days.

Heat rash If she's too warm, your baby may get small red spots, particularly on her face. Make sure that she isn't too warmly wrapped in clothing and blankets, and that you can regulate the temperature of her room (see pp. 81 and 82).

Urticaria (hives) This is a kind of itchy rash in which the spots have a white centre and a red halo. It is quite common in the first week, and it may recur for a month or so. There is no need for treatment; it will disappear quite quickly.

YOUR BABY'S APPEARANCE

When you hold your baby for the first time, her appearance will probably surprise you. She's undoubtedly a joy to you, but you may have expected a clean and placid bundle, similar to the babies that appear in baby-food commercials. Real life (as you'll now suddenly discover) is a bit different.

Skin A whitish, greasy substance – vernix – may cover your baby's skin. This natural barrier cream prevented the skin from becoming waterlogged in the uterus. It may be removed at once, or left to give your baby some natural protection against minor skin irritations such as flaking and peeling.

Blotchy skin is due to the tiny blood vessels being unstable. Black children are often light-skinned at birth, but the skin darkens as it begins to produce melanin, its natural pigment; it will reach its permanent colour by about six months.

Head Your baby's skull is made up of four large plates that haven't yet fused. This allows them to move across each other so that your baby can pass through the birth canal without hazard. Her head may get slightly elongated or misshapen in the process; this is normal and doesn't affect the brain. Any swelling or bruising disappears in the first few days or weeks.

The soft spots on the top of your baby's skull where the bones are still not joined are called the fontanelles. In a sense, they are the windows into a baby's body. The skull bones won't fuse completely until your baby is about two. You may be able to see a faint pulse beating beneath her scalp.

Eyes Your baby may not be able to open her eyes straight away due to puffiness caused by pressure on her head during birth. This may also have broken some tiny blood vessels in her eyes, causing harmless small, red, triangular marks in the whites that need no treatment and disappear in a couple of weeks. She may have "sticky eye" – a yellow discharge around the eyelids. This is quite common, and although not serious should always be treated by a doctor.

Your baby may squint or look cross-eyed because although she can see clearly to a distance of 20 centimetres (8 inches) or so, she cannot focus both eyes at the same time beyond that. These conditions clear up as her eye muscles grow stronger (usually within a month); consult a doctor if she still squints at three months. If she is reluctant to open her eyes at first, never force them open. Try holding her above your head so that she opens them naturally. Most newborns have blue eyes. The colour is likely to change after birth, since this is when a baby acquires melanin, the body's natural pigment.

Hair Some babies are born with a full head of hair; others are completely bald. The colour of your baby's hair at birth may not be the colour she will end up with later on. The fine downy hair that many babies have on their bodies at birth is called lanugo, and this will fall off soon after birth.

Genitals Many babies of both sexes appear to have enlarged genitals and "breasts" shortly after birth. This is due to the massive increase in hormone levels that you've experienced just before giving birth, some of which have passed into your baby's bloodstream. A baby boy may develop an enlarged scrotum and enlarged breasts; he may even produce a little milk. This is not abnormal, and the swelling will gradually subside. A baby girl may have a swollen vulva or clitoris and a small "period" shortly after birth.

Umbilicus The umbilical cord, which is moist and bluish-white at birth, is clamped with forceps and then cut with scissors. Only a short length of cord remains, and this will dry up and become almost black within two to four hours. The stump will shrivel up and fall off after about seven days, but your baby will feel no pain at all.

UMBILICAL HERNIA

Some babies develop a small swelling near the navel, called an umbilical hernia. This is caused when the abdominal muscles are weak, allowing the intestines to push through a little, which creates a bulge.

An umbilical hernia is most obvious when the abdominal muscles are used for crying. It is a very common occurrence, and virtually always clears up within a year. If your baby has one and it enlarges or persists, be sure to consult your doctor.

Site of swelling
The hernia forms where the umbilical cord entered the baby's abdomen, because at that point there is a gap in the abdominal muscles.

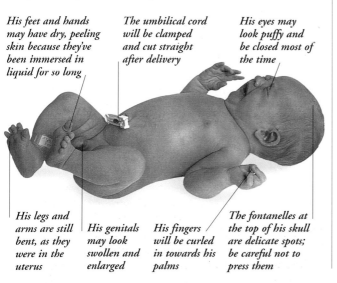

His feet and hands may have dry, peeling skin because they've been immersed in liquid for so long

The umbilical cord will be clamped and cut straight after delivery

His eyes may look puffy and be closed most of the time

His legs and arms are still bent, as they were in the uterus

His genitals may look swollen and enlarged

His fingers will be curled in towards his palms

The fontanelles at the top of his skull are delicate spots; be careful not to press them

ABOUT BIRTHMARKS

If you haven't found a single blemish anywhere on your baby's body, you probably haven't looked long enough.

Virtually every child is born with some kind of birthmark. Most will fade and disappear by the time your child is three, but some will remain and increase in size.

Both my sons had stork-bite birthmarks at the back of the neck just under the hairline, a very common place to find them. The marks disappeared by the time the babies were six months old.

You might find a stork-bite anywhere, including on the neck, forehead and eyelids.

Superficial birthmarks do no harm, are nothing to worry about and need no treatment.

Measurements
The circumference of your baby's head will be measured as well as his length. He will also be weighed.

MEASUREMENTS

Your baby's weight, head circumference, and length will be measured to see how mature she is, and as a useful baseline for her development. Inevitably, they'll be compared to the "average", yet an average is just an arithmetical calculation: the "average child" is only theoretical and doesn't exist.

Weight The range for babies born around their expected time is 2.4–4.8 kilograms (5 pounds 4 ounces to 10 pounds 8 ounces). If you're tall, heavy or diabetic, your baby may be on the heavy side. Women with chronic hypertension, vascular or renal disease or pre-eclampsia, or who smoke during pregnancy are likely to have lighter babies. A baby born at less than 40 weeks is also likely to be lighter. Girls generally weigh slightly less than boys; twins or other multiple births weigh less than singletons.

It is normal for your baby to lose weight in the first few days after birth as her body adjusts to new feeding requirements. She must now process her own food, and it will take a while for her to feed consistently. The usual weight loss at this time is about 115–170 grams (4–6 ounces). After a few days, you can expect your baby's weight to begin increasing.

A baby's weight gain tells us a great deal about her overall physical health. Steady weight gain indicates that her food intake is sufficient and that food is being absorbed; poor or erratic weight gain or weight loss signals that food intake is insufficient or that food isn't being properly absorbed.

Head circumference Your baby's head is disproportionately large to her body size; it is one-quarter of her length. The younger a baby is, the larger her head is in proportion to her body. The average circumference of a newborn baby's head is about 35 centimetres (14 inches). Measuring head circumference is regarded as a vital part of examining a baby because the growth of the head reflects the development of the brain; some experts think that there's a direct relationship between the circumference of the head and intelligence. An unusually large or small head circumference may indicate an abnormality of the brain.

Chest and abdomen The circumference of your baby's chest will be smaller than that of her head. Her stomach might look very large, and even distended, but given the weakness of her abdominal muscles, this is to be expected.

THE FIRST NAPPIES

Your baby's stools and urine may not look as you expect. If you have a baby girl, there may be some vaginal discharge. None of this necessarily means that something is wrong.

Stools Your baby's first bowel movement (which should be passed within the first 24 hours) consists of blackish green meconium, which is mainly digested mucus. It's not unusual for her next bowel movement to be two days later, especially if you are breastfeeding (check that your baby is wetting her nappy regularly, however). After the fourth day, she may pass four or five motions daily. You'll notice that the colour and composition of her stools change from the first blackish-green to greenish-brown, and then to a yellow semi-solid kind. If you are bottlefeeding your baby, the stools might resemble scrambled eggs.

Most babies fill their nappies as soon as they have eaten. This is due to a perfectly healthy reflex that makes the bowel empty itself as soon as food enters the stomach. Some babies pass motions much more infrequently, but as long as your baby does not have to strain and her motions are a normal colour and soft, there's no need for you to be concerned. If her motions are infrequent or hard, it's a good idea to give her a small amount of water (15 millilitres or one tablespoon) two or three times a day.

Urine Newborns pass urine almost continuously because the bladder muscles are underdeveloped. Your baby may not be able to hold urine for any length of time (usually no longer than a few minutes), so it's normal to find that she wets her nappy up to 20 times in 24 hours. When she does, her urine will contain substances called urates that may stain her nappy dark pink or red. This, too, is normal for a newborn.

Vaginal discharge Newborn girls sometimes produce a clear or white vaginal discharge. A small amount of vaginal bleeding can sometimes occur, but this is perfectly normal and will clear up naturally after a couple of days. If you are really worried, consult your doctor for reassurance.

COMMON BIRTHMARKS

Most birthmarks are simply abnormal collections of small blood vessels under the skin. They are harmless and do not cause your baby any pain.

Strawberry marks Usually first seen as small, sometimes inconspicuous, red dots, these may grow alarmingly into red raised lumps during the first months. They shrivel and disappear in the second year without leaving a scar.

Salmon patches Also called stork's marks or stork-bites, these pink discolorations of the skin usually fade with time, often within a few months.

Spider birthmarks (naevi) These small marks appear soon after birth as either a network or a cobweb of dilated vessels. They generally disappear after the first year.

Pigmented naevi These brownish patches can occur anywhere on the body. They're usually pale and nearly always enlarge as the child grows, but they seldom become darker.

Port wine stains Dilated capillaries in the skin cause these bright red or even purple marks, found on any part of the body. They are permanent, but can be removed with laser treatment or camouflaged with specially formulated make-up.

Mongolian spots Dark bluish-black discolorations, usually on the buttocks or back, are often seen on dark-skinned babies. These will fade naturally.

EYE REFLEXES

Your baby will close her eyes, blink, or move them from side to side, depending on what is happening around her.

- *If light shines in her face, she will blink, usually whether she has her eyes open or not (you should never shine bright light directly in your baby's eyes).*

- *She will also blink if you tap the bridge of her nose or blow gently across her eyes, or if she is startled by a sudden noise.*

- *If you lift your newborn up and turn her to the left or right, her eyes will not usually move to the left or right, but will stay fixed in the same position momentarily. This is called the "doll's-eye response", and will normally disappear after about ten days.*

NEWBORN BEHAVIOUR

Once your baby is born, it may take you a while to get used to her behaviour. It is worth taking the time to study her reactions to various stimuli, and becoming familiar with some of the traits that will mark her personality. Young babies have far more individuality than they are usually credited with, and this is a useful fact to bear in mind as you get to know your child.

REFLEXES

One thing common to all healthy babies is a number of reflexes that can be stimulated from the very first moments after birth. These reflexes are unconscious movements that eventually – at about three months – start to be replaced by conscious movements.

You might notice that your newborn baby responds in a positive way to your presence by momentarily contracting the whole of her face and body. As she starts learning to

Grasp reflex
If you put something in the palm of your baby's hand, he will clench it surprisingly tightly. The grasp of a baby is often tight enough to support his entire body weight (although you should never try this).

He instinctively opens his mouth to suck your finger

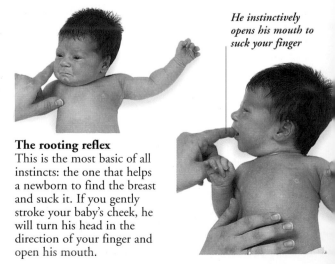

Moro reflex
When your baby's head is allowed to drop back, he will throw his limbs up with fingers outstretched, then let them fall back slowly towards his body.

The rooting reflex
This is the most basic of all instincts: the one that helps a newborn to find the breast and suck it. If you gently stroke your baby's cheek, he will turn his head in the direction of your finger and open his mouth.

control her movements, you will notice that her reactions become more directed and less random. For instance, at six weeks, instead of scrunching up her whole face, she may show you a distinct smile.

TESTING REFLEXES

Until your baby's physical and mental capabilities develop, it will be her instinctive reflexes that provide an indication of her maturity. Doctors can test these reflexes to check your baby's general health and see that her central nervous system is functioning properly and well. Premature babies will not react in the same way as full-term babies.

Although there are more than 70 primitive, unconscious reflexes that have been identified in newborn babies, your doctor is likely to test only a selected few. The two most commonly recognized reflexes that are easy to test yourself are the grasp and rooting reflexes (see left). Don't attempt to test the Moro reflex (see far left) at home, because this could distress your baby and make her cry.

Walking reflex

If you hold your baby under the shoulders so that he is in an upright position and his feet are allowed to touch a firm surface, he'll move his legs in a walking action. This reflex disappears in three to six weeks, and is not what helps your child learn to walk.

Stepping reflex

This is quite similar to the walking reflex. If you hold your baby in an upright position and bring the front of his leg into contact with the edge of a table, he will lift his foot as if to step onto the table. The same reflex is in the arms: if the back of your baby's forearm touches the edge of the table, he will raise his arm as if to grasp it.

"Crawling"

When you place your baby on his stomach, he will automatically assume what appears to be a crawling position, with his pelvis high and knees pulled up under his abdomen. When he kicks his legs, he may be able to shuffle in a vague "crawling" manner. It is not real crawling, however, and this behaviour will disappear as soon as his legs uncurl and he lies flat.

Your baby takes up a "crawling" position when placed on his stomach

YOUR NEWBORN GIRL

As soon as she is born, you can observe in your baby many behavioural traits that are typical of girls.

- *Hearing in girls is very acute and they can be calmed down with soothing words much more readily than boys.*

- *If a baby girl hears another baby crying, she cries for longer than a boy would.*

- *Baby girls use their own voice to get their mother's attention earlier and more often than boys.*

- *Baby girls have no difficulty in locating a sound's source.*

- *Girls respond enthusiastically to visual stimulation right from the moment of birth.*

- *Baby girls are interested in everything that is unusual.*

- *Girls prefer the human face to almost anything else. Later in life, this trait shows as an intuitive ability to read facial expression, regardless of any cultural differences.*

COPING WITH CRYING

Assume that your baby will cry a lot and it may be a pleasant surprise if she doesn't. If you think she won't cry and she does, you may find yourself overwhelmed and disoriented.

Remember that there are really only three states your newborn baby can be in: asleep, awake and quiet, or awake and crying. If she is crying, there are a variety of reasons for it. The most likely causes are tiredness, hunger, loneliness and discomfort – she is too hot or too cold, in an uncomfortable position, or needs changing. You must accept sometimes, however, that a baby will cry for no apparent reason. This type of crying can be the most stressful for a parent.

Responding to crying Leaving a child to cry alone is never a good idea, even though you will hear this advice often. If a baby is denied attention and friendship in her early weeks and months, she may grow up to be withdrawn and shy. Research on newborns shows that if parents are slow to respond to their baby's crying, the result may be a baby that cries more rather than less. One study found that babies whose crying was ignored in their first few weeks tended to cry more frequently and persistently as they grew older.

Often people confuse spoiling a child with loving a child. In my opinion a baby cannot be "spoiled" enough. A six-month-old baby who is picked up, nursed, cuddled, and talked to soothingly and lovingly is not learning about seeking attention; she is learning about love and forming human relationships – and that is one of the most important lessons a child will ever learn in terms of future emotional and psychological development. What we tend to call spoiling is both the natural response of a mother to a distressed child, and the natural need of her baby.

SLEEP PATTERNS AND NEEDS

Once you bring your baby home, you'll have some sleepless nights unless you are very lucky. Although most newborns usually sleep when they're not feeding, typically spending at least 60 percent of their time asleep, some stay active and alert for surprisingly long periods during the day and night.

One young mother was shocked to find that her new baby never dozed for longer than one or two hours at a time until she was four months old. This is a very long time for any parent to last without a full night's sleep, especially when your body may be in need of rest after an exhausting pregnancy and birth. If your baby is very wakeful, take consolation in knowing that as long as she isn't left bored on her own, every minute of being awake she's learning something new – and in the long run you will be rewarded with an eager, bright child.

All babies are different, and their requirements for sleep depend on individual make-up. For this reason it makes no sense to lay down rigid sleeping times that correspond to the "average" baby; the average baby just doesn't exist.

Most newborns fall asleep soon after feeding. At first, a baby's wakefulness is likely to depend on how much feeding she needs, which in turn depends on her weight.

SOUNDS YOUR BABY MAKES

Whether asleep or awake, babies make a variety of strange noises, and this is quite normal. Most of them are due to the immaturity of the respiratory system and will soon disappear.

Snoring Your baby may make some grunting noises when she's asleep. This is not a true snore, and is probably caused by vibrations on the soft palate at the back of her mouth as she breathes in and out.

Snuffling Your baby may snuffle so loudly with each breath that you think she has a cold, or catarrh at the back of her throat. In most babies, these snuffling noises are harmless and are caused because the bridge of the nose is low, and air is trying to get through very short, narrow nasal passages. As your baby grows older, the bridge of her nose will get higher and the snuffling sound will gradually disappear.

Sneezing You may also think your baby has a cold because she sneezes a lot. In fact, sneezing is common in newborn babies, particularly if they open their eyes and are exposed to bright light. This sneezing can actually be beneficial – it helps clear out your baby's nasal passages.

Hiccups Newborn babies hiccup a lot, particularly after a feed. This leads some mothers to fear that their baby has indigestion, but this is rarely so. Hiccups are due to imperfect control of the diaphragm (the sheet of muscle that separates the chest from the abdomen) and they will disappear as your baby's control of the diaphragm matures.

YOUR NEWBORN BOY

From the moment of birth, baby boys show characteristic male behaviour, some of which will persist throughout life.

- *Hearing in boys is less acute than in girls, so boys are more difficult to calm down.*

- *If a newborn boy hears another baby cry, he'll join in but stop crying quite quickly.*

- *Baby boys don't make sounds when they hear their mother's voice early on. This slow response lasts throughout life.*

- *Newborn boys find it difficult to locate the source of sounds.*

- *Baby boys need more visual stimulation than girls. They quickly lose interest in a design or picture, and lag behind girls in visual maturity up to the age of seven months.*

- *Baby boys are interested in the differences between things.*

- *Boys are more active, and are interested in things just as much as in people.*

- *Boys want to taste and touch everything, and move things about more than girls.*

APGAR SCALE

Immediately after birth, your baby will be given five short tests to assess her health. Each test is scored either 0, 1 or 2. A total of over 7 means she is in good condition. Under 4 means she needs help, and will receive resuscitation. Most low-scoring babies score highly when re-tested a few minutes later. The tests are:

Appearance *A pink skin colour shows that her lungs are working well.*

Pulse *This shows how strong and regular her heartbeat is.*

Grimace/crying *Facial expressions and responses show how alert she is to stimuli.*

Activity *Moving her limbs shows the health of her muscles.*

Respiration *Breathing shows the health of her lungs.*

Grimace

Pulse

Respiration

Appearance

Activity

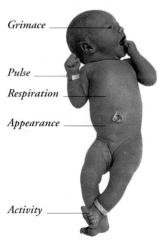

Assessing a newborn
The baby is checked to make sure that her lungs and heart are working properly and her responses are healthy.

NEWBORN HEALTH

Whether you give birth in hospital or at home, the doctor or midwife will see that your baby gets expert uninterrupted attention until breathing is well established. Major problems should be identified in minutes so that any special care can begin as early as possible. Immediately after delivery, the doctor or midwife will test your baby against the Apgar scale (see left), and then examine her to assess her general condition. The sort of checks your doctor will do involve:

- Making sure that she has normal facial features and that her body proportions are normal.
- Turning her over to see that her back is normal and that there is no spina bifida (a condition in which the coverings of the brain and spinal cord are left exposed).
- Examining her anus, legs, fingers and toes.
- Recording the number of blood vessels in the umbilical cord (normally there are two arteries and one vein).
- Weighing her.
- Measuring her head and body length.
- Checking her temperature with a rectal thermometer and warming her if she needs it.

An experienced doctor or midwife can do these preliminary checks in less than a minute. You will then be able to rest easy, knowing that your baby is healthy and normal.

WHAT HAPPENS THE NEXT DAY

Once all the initial tests have been carried out and you have held and suckled your baby for as long as you and your partner want, she will be wrapped up snugly and put in her cot to keep warm. She'll be given a thorough examination 24 hours later to ensure that all is well. This takes place when your baby is warm and relaxed. Ask the hospital staff to let you know when the doctor is going to perform the examination so that you can be there. This will give you the opportunity to ask your doctor questions and to discuss any worries that you may have at this stage.

Your baby will be placed on a flat surface, in a good light and at a convenient height for the doctor, who may be seated. If you're immobile, you can have the examination at your bedside; if you cannot be there for some reason, always make sure to get the results. Your doctor will generally start examining at the top of the head and work down to the toes.

Head and neck The doctor will look at the skull bones and fontanelles (see p. 12) and check for any misshaping that occurred when the head passed through the birth canal. He will look at the eyes, ears and nose; check the mouth for cleft palate, or any other abnormality, and teeth (they are rare but not unknown); and check the neck for cysts or swellings.

Chest and heart The doctor will use a stethoscope to check the lungs and heart, which should be expanded and working normally. When your baby becomes responsible for her circulation, the heart's workload increases and odd sounds occur, heard as a heart murmur. Most go away spontaneously and quickly. Your baby will be examined during the post-natal check-up to see if a heart murmur persists.

Arms and hands The doctor will check either arm for a pulse, and for normal movement and strength. He will also check the fingers and palm creases. Nearly all babies have two major creases across each palm; if there is only one, he will look for other physical abnormalities.

Abdomen and genitals The doctor will gently press your baby's abdomen to check the size and shape of the liver and spleen (in newborns, both may be slightly enlarged). He will check a boy's testes to ensure that they are properly descended and a girl's labia to see that they are not joined and that the clitoris is a normal size. He will also check the lower spine and anus for congenital abnormalities.

Hips, legs and feet The doctor will hold both thighs firmly and move each leg to see if the head of the thigh bone is unstable or lies outside the hip joint, suggesting congenital dislocation of the hip. (Testing the hips is not painful, but the movement may make your baby cry.) The doctor will examine her legs and feet to make sure they are of equal size and length. If the ankle is still turned inwards as it was in the uterus, your baby may have a club foot. This can be treated with manipulation and perhaps a cast.

Nerves and muscles The doctor will manipulate your baby's arms and legs to make sure they are not too stiff or floppy. This tells him the health of her nerves and muscles. He will make sure that the normal newborn reflexes are present (see pp. 16 and 17), and check your baby's head control.

JAUNDICE

This is not a disease and, in the majority of newborn babies, is not dangerous.

Jaundice is likely to occur when a baby is about three days old. It is caused when red blood cells break down shortly after birth, creating an excess of a pigment (bilirubin) in the blood. This pigment gives the baby's skin a yellowish tinge.

A newborn baby cannot excrete the bilirubin rapidly enough to prevent jaundice until her liver is more mature, at about one week. Treatment for jaundice is usually just a short spell (about 12 hours) under an ultraviolet light; but even without this, the condition should clear up by itself within a week.

A more serious type of jaundice can appear if mother and baby have incompatible blood types (usually a Rhesus-negative mother with a Rhesus-positive baby). This needs treatment within the first two days. If your blood type is found to be incompatible with that of your baby, all your medical staff will have taken preventive steps before you give birth.

Hepatitis and biliary atresia (a rare condition in which the baby's bile duct fails to develop properly) are other, less common, causes of jaundice.

YOUR PARTNER

In many households, the father becomes the main helper when his partner comes home with their new baby. Some men immediately involve themselves in caring for their partner and child, but those who do not need prompting into action.

At this time, what you need from your partner more than anything else is understanding, sympathy and a readiness to let his routine relax and go along with you and the baby. This needs serious discussion before the baby is born – otherwise your partner may find it hard to adapt and may also feel neglected, inadequate and bereft of your usual affection and attention.

You may find it useful to divide up the work between you. For instance, your partner could take over the cleaning, shopping and laundry, leaving you free to concentrate on looking after yourself and the baby. Or you could simply share all the work of looking after your home and child.

ARRANGING CHILDCARE

During the last weeks of pregnancy, it's a good idea for you and your partner to spend time discussing and planning how you are going to run your domestic routine once you settle down at home with your new child. If your partner is both willing and able to play a full part (or if he can be encouraged to do so), you should be able to cope without too much difficulty; if not, you should get someone in to help you, especially for the first few weeks.

The first few days of motherhood will be harder than you think. Labour and birth are physically and emotionally draining; you'll feel you have very few reserves, and you will also be extremely fatigued. You will realize, once you are at home with your baby, that one job or activity succeeds another almost without respite, and in the middle of all this activity you are still learning about being a mother. Even if you have read every baby book going, you will find that your baby conforms to no typical schedule or plan, and that you have to work out your life around your baby's routine. It is a mistake to try to impose a routine on your baby, and will only cause you more work; you have to take your lead from her. As far as your sleep is concerned, get it when you can: new babies don't know night from day and need the same attention during the night as during the day.

In the first few weeks at home with your baby, try to get someone else to be responsible for all the household chores, or simply cut back the amount and what you do to the bare minimum, until you become used to the schedule that your baby follows naturally.

Look at your baby while feeding her

Enjoyable mealtime help
If you are breastfeeding, express milk into a bottle (see pp. 42–3) so that your partner also has the pleasure of feeding the baby.

SOURCES OF HELP

Unless you want to become extremely tired, even depressed and weepy, you will need some help to tide you over at least the first few days with your baby, and preferably the first week or two. Don't be too proud to ask for or accept help; if you are too reticent, you may soon come to regret it. Having someone help out does not mean that you are in any way inadequate as a mother. The best possible solution is some live-in help, so that your day can be split into shifts. That way, you can at least make sure that you get sufficient rest and pay attention to your diet.

Family and friends Your mother and your mother-in-law are probably the people you trust most in the world when it comes to childcare. They have had children of their own and are experienced at looking after babies, and they will give you lots of helpful support and advice. A good idea would be to ask one of them (or a sister, other relative or friend) to come and live in your house around the time you expect to go into labour. That way, she can become familiar with the routine you have established in your home with your family and partner, and be ready to receive and help you when you come home with the baby.

Such a helper is invaluable. You will feel confident that your household is ticking over quite normally. She should take off your shoulders all the administration and see to meals, laundry, shopping and so on. This can relieve some of the responsibility from your partner, so you will both be able to devote more time to your baby. In addition, if your helper has had children of her own, she can be a fountain of information and welcome advice.

Nannies If you decide that you would like a nanny, try to arrange for her to be settled in with your family before the baby is born. This is a very good idea because it gives you time to get to know each other. You will develop a sense of rapport (or not, as the case may be) and you should be able to tell whether or not you are going to get on together. Having a newborn baby in the house is quite a traumatic event, and it is important to have a helper who will fit in with your routines and adapt to your lifestyle. You must also have confidence in her abilities and feel happy with her relationship with your baby.

MATERNITY NURSES

If you want short-term, live-in help, consider hiring a maternity nurse. She will join your household just before or after the baby is born and will help you with all of the babycare.

As well as providing welcome help with the baby, maternity nurses are invaluable teachers. They will show you how to take care of your baby's daily needs: how to change nappies; how to breast- or bottlefeed her, how to know when your baby's had enough and how to take the baby carefully off your breast to avoid soreness and cracked nipples, for example.

But it's up to you and your maternity nurse to work out what kind of a regime you would like. You may decide, for instance, that you wish to have an uninterrupted night's sleep; the nurse will be on duty all the way through the night but you will take over at, say, 7 a.m. so that she can get some rest. Later on in the day, she would be responsible for the baby's laundry, preparation of formula feeding, keeping the nursery clean, and looking after all the baby's needs and some of yours too.

A maternity nurse usually does not stay in your home for more than 4 weeks – but you can arrange for her to stay for longer if your finances can stretch to it. Maternity nurses are expensive, but hiring one will get you off to a good start if there is no-one else to help.

By far the best way to find a nanny is through the personal recommendation of a trusted friend. The second best way is through a really reliable nanny agency. Not all of them are reliable, and I recommend you contact the Federation of Recruitment and Employment Services for the most reliable one in your area. Very high-class nanny agencies are not necessarily the best, and you will pay more for your nanny from one of these than from other agencies.

Advertising for a nanny is another option. But no matter how you recruit your nanny, it is absolutely essential that you see her at least twice before you hire her. On the first occasion you could have a formal interview, and on the second you could relax over some lunch or tea or maybe go shopping together. By doing this you will learn more about her, get a clearer picture of her personality, and be able to judge whether you will actually get on together.

Draw up some kind of employment contract in which you cover the important aspects of the job, including the required approaches and attitudes. Make certain any tasks are carefully and clearly laid out; make it plain that instant dismissal may follow if your instructions are not followed. Your nanny should be prepared to bend her usual practices in order to adapt to and fit in with yours, but it would be pointless hiring someone who is a strict disciplinarian if you want your children to be brought up in a liberal and laid-back manner. Only you know, however, exactly how you want your baby treated, so you must discuss each and every one of your relevant likes and dislikes (however trivial they may seem) with your prospective nanny.

Au pairs These young women (or occasionally young men) from abroad will help you with your baby in exchange for room, board and a small wage. An au pair is cheaper than a nanny, but bear in mind that most will probably have no training in childcare, and may speak little English.

2

HOLDING
AND
COMFORTING

If your baby seems very vulnerable to you in the
first few weeks of life, be reassured that this feeling
is common: many parents are rather anxious
about picking up their newborns, fearful that they
may somehow damage their child.
Children benefit from physical contact – in fact,
the need for physical affection is something you
never outgrow – so come to terms with holding your
baby confidently for his sake as well as your own.

PUTTING YOUR BABY DOWN

For the first three months of his life, you should always lay your baby on his back.

Research in recent years has demonstrated that babies who sleep on their fronts are at greater risk of cot death than babies placed on their backs, and publicity in the UK about this finding has resulted in a reduction in cot deaths of almost 50 percent in five years.

HANDLING AND CARRYING

A newborn baby may appear very vulnerable and fragile, but he is a good deal more robust than you might think. With this knowledge uppermost in your mind, you will be able to inspire confidence rather than uncertainty in your child. For the baby's comfort, and for your own peace of mind, you must feel at ease when you handle him; you must be able to hold your baby confidently in order to bathe, dress and feed him successfully.

HANDLING YOUR BABY

When you move your baby, the action must be as slow, gentle and quiet as possible. You'll find that you instinctively hold your baby close, look into his eyes, and talk soothingly to him. Not surprisingly, it has been proven that all children benefit from close physical contact, particularly when they can hear the familiar sound of your heartbeat. Premature babies, for example, gain more weight when they are laid on fleecy sheets, which give them the sensation of being touched, than when they are laid on smooth ones. Your newborn baby will find comfort in any kind of skin-to-skin contact, but the best way to give him this is for both of you to lie naked in bed. Here he can smell and feel your skin, and hear your heartbeat. In this way, too, you can make sure that he becomes familiar with the smell of his father's skin.

HOW TO PICK UP YOUR BABY

Lifting your baby
Slide one hand under your baby's neck and the other hand under his back and bottom to support his lower body securely. Pick him up gently and smoothly, then transfer him to a carrying position.

Whenever you pick up and put down your baby, make sure to support his head: he has little control over it until he's about four weeks old. If his head flops back, he'll feel that he's going to fall, his body will jerk, and he'll stretch out his arms and legs in the Moro, or "startle", reflex (see p. 16).

Put down and pick up your baby with your whole arm supporting his spine, neck and head. Swaddling your baby tightly makes him feel secure; it's a useful way to comfort a distressed baby. Wrap him firmly in a shawl or blanket so that his head is supported and his arms are close against his body. Once you lay him in the cot, unwrap him gently.

TWO WAYS TO CARRY YOUR BABY

Carry your baby in your arms by cradling his head in the crook of one slightly inclined arm. The rest of his body will rest on the lower part of your arm, encircled by your wrist and hand, which support his back and bottom. Your other arm provides additional support to his bottom and legs, and your baby can see your face as you talk to and smile at him.

Alternatively, hold your baby against your upper chest with his head on your shoulder. Place your forearm across his back, with your hand supporting his resting head and the other hand free. Use your free hand to support your baby's bottom, or to help you balance. Your sense of balance will change at first as you get used to carrying your new baby.

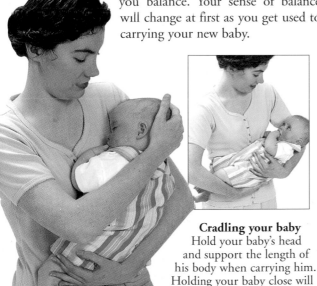

Cradling your baby
Hold your baby's head and support the length of his body when carrying him. Holding your baby close will make him feel safe, especially if he can see your face.

CARRYING YOUR BABY IN A SLING

Newborns are best carried in lightweight slings worn on the chest, where they feel close to you and secure.

● *Choose a sling in a washable fabric, since it will inevitably get rather dirty as you carry your baby around.*

● *The sling must be easy to put on and comfortable to wear for both you and your partner. Try it out with your baby before you decide to buy it.*

● *The sling you choose should give good support to your baby's head and neck, and keep him secure; he must not be able to slip out of the sides.*

● *The shoulder straps must be wide enough to support your growing baby's weight. Wide shoulder straps will also make carrying more comfortable.*

● *It has been said that a baby shouldn't be carried in a sling until he can support his own head. This is not true. Use a sling as soon as you and your baby are comfortable with it.*

BENEFITS FOR
PARENTS

BABY MASSAGE

Massage is a delightful and valuable activity that has advantages for you and your partner as well as your baby.

• *Massaging your newborn baby helps to enhance the bonding process between you and your child.*

• *If you are anxious or have had little experience with children, massage allows you to get used to handling your new baby with confidence.*

• *Massage is an ideal way to soothe an unsettled baby and can also help to calm your nerves with its relaxing effects.*

• *You'll find that massaging your baby's soft, smooth skin is a sensual and comforting experience for both of you.*

Massage can have all the benefits for a baby that it has for an adult; it is soothing and can calm a fretful baby, and is a marvellous way of showing love. If you massage your baby every day he will learn to recognize the routine and will show pleasure as you begin. You can continue to massage your baby as he gets older; a massage is often the ideal way to calm and soothe an excited toddler.

Provide a relaxed atmosphere before you start. Since this will be a new experience for you both, any distractions can spoil the mood and upset your baby, so choose a time when there is no-one else around and unplug the phone. Make sure the room is nice and comfortably warm, and lay your baby on a warm towel or sheepskin, or on your lap. Work from his head down, using light, even strokes, and ensure that both sides of his body are massaged symmetrically. Make eye contact with your baby throughout the massage and talk quietly, gently and lovingly to him.

GIVING A MASSAGE

Head and face
Using a circular motion, lightly massage the crown of your baby's head, then stroke down the sides of his face. Massage his forehead, working from the centre out; move over his eyebrows and cheeks to finish around his ears.

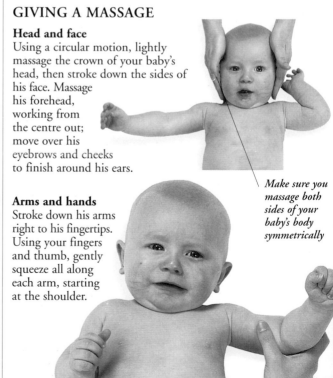

Make sure you massage both sides of your baby's body symmetrically

Arms and hands
Stroke down his arms right to his fingertips. Using your fingers and thumb, gently squeeze all along each arm, starting at the shoulder.

Neck and shoulders
Gently massage your baby's neck from his ears down to his shoulders, and from his chin to his chest. Then stroke his shoulders from his neck outwards.

Chest and abdomen

Gently stroke down your baby's chest, following the delicate curves of his ribs with your fingers. Rub his abdomen in a circular motion and work in a clockwise direction from the navel outwards.

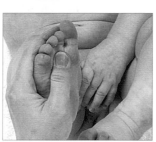

Feet and toes

Massage your baby's ankles and feet, stroking from heel to toe, and then concentrate on each toe individually. Finish massaging his front with some long, light strokes up and down the whole length of his body (make sure to go gently over his navel and abdomen).

Legs and ankles

Now you can massage your baby's legs, working from his thighs down to his knees. Stroke down the shins, and move around to his calves and ankles. Gently squeeze all the way down.

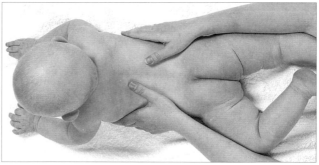

Massaging your baby's back

Once you have finished massaging your baby on the front, turn him over and work gently on his back.

CRYING GIRLS AND BOYS

Girl and boy babies differ in why and how much they cry, and in how they respond to attempts to soothe them.

- *Baby girls are less vulnerable to stress at the time of birth than boys, and less likely to cry.*

- *Girls are less likely than boys to cry in new situations; boys tend to take longer to adapt.*

- *Mothers tend to give extra attention to girls who cry a lot.*

- *Boys cry more readily than girls if parental attention and love are not forthcoming.*

- *Boys are less likely to get extra attention when they cry a lot: their mothers mistakenly want them to be tough.*

Good communication
The only way your baby can make his needs known is by crying, so always respond.

CRYING AND COMFORTING

All babies cry quite a lot and yours will too, so be prepared for it. There will be times when the reason for his crying is obvious and easily remedied: he's hungry, too hot, too cold, bored, uncomfortable because of a wet or a dirty nappy, or he might simply want your closeness and affection. One reason for crying that parents often fail to recognize is the desire for sleep. I well remember trying to console my newborn son in all kinds of ways before it occurred to me that he just wanted to be left alone to sleep.

Very young babies cry when they are disturbed, when roughly handled, for instance at bathtime, or when they get a shock – perhaps from feeling that they are going to be dropped, from a loud noise or from a bright light. A two-week-old baby always responds to the security of being firmly wrapped in a shawl or held in strong and confident arms. Once you have investigated your baby's crying, don't worry too much about it – crying is practically his only way of communicating his needs to you.

Recognizing different cries Within a few weeks, you can distinguish between the different cries that mean your baby is hungry, is niggling because he is bored, wants to be put down to sleep or just wants a cuddle. Your baby is learning about you and how to communicate with you too. He cries out of need and you respond by giving him what he wants.

RESPONDING TO YOUR BABY

I believe you should respond quite quickly to your baby's cry. If you don't respond, then your baby feels just as you would if you were being ignored in a conversation. There is a considerable amount of research to show that your baby is affected by how you respond when he is crying. For instance, mothers who respond quickly to crying are likely to have children with greater and more advanced communication skills, including speaking and outgoing behaviour. Babies who are ignored cry more often and for longer in the first year than babies who are attended to quickly. It seems that mothers cause

CRYING AND COMFORTING

their babies to settle into a pattern of crying often and persistently because they fail to respond, and a vicious circle is set up in which the baby cries, the mother fails to respond, the baby cries more and the mother is even less inclined to act. A sensitive response promotes self-confidence and self-esteem in your child's later life. Some mothers believe that always responding will "spoil" their babies. A young baby has a limitless capacity for soaking up love: there's no way that you can spoil a baby by attention in his first year.

CRYING SPELLS

Most babies have crying spells. Often crying occurs in the late afternoon or early evening, when your baby may cry for as long as half an hour. If your baby has colic (see p. 33), evening crying spells can last up to two hours. At one time mothers used to say that a child required this exercise to help develop healthy lungs and therefore felt they could leave their babies to cry. This is nonsense; you should always try to console your baby during a crying spell.

Once your child establishes a pattern of crying spells they may go on for several weeks. It's understandable – it's your baby's way of becoming adjusted to being in a very different world from that experienced inside your uterus. The more sensitively you respond to him and take your lead from him, the more rapidly he will become acclimatized to his new lifestyle; the sooner you accommodate his likes and dislikes, the sooner crying spells will stop.

NIGHT-TIME CRYING

There is no doubt that every parent finds crying spells hard to cope with, especially at night. Don't get frustrated because your child doesn't respond to your attempts to soothe him. If walking up and down, singing songs or swaddling just don't seem to work, you could take him for a short drive; the gentle swaying motion of a car may send him to sleep.

During the night, crying will almost certainly make you feel impatient at the least, and at the worst, that you will do anything to stop your baby crying. These feelings are quite normal, so don't become frightened and tense – otherwise the crying will simply get worse. When my five-day-old baby cried persistently during the night, I actually thought that if I threw him against the wall he would be bound to stop. I didn't, of course, but it is quite normal to think such things; it would have been abnormal only if I had done it.

IF YOUR BABY CRIES A LOT

Research shows that your child may cry despite your best efforts to console him.

• *Babies of mothers who have a general anaesthetic during labour, or who have been delivered by forceps, tend to cry more in the first weeks of life.*

• *Babies born after a long labour are likely to sleep in short bursts, and to cry quite a lot between sleeps.*

• *If you are tense, irritable and impatient, you will undoubtedly communicate your mood to your baby, who will sense it and cry.*

• *Babies from different races are not the same. For instance, European-American babies cry more than Chinese-American babies, even when given the same care and attention.*

DUMMIES

Babies are born with a sucking reflex. Without it, they wouldn't suckle or be able to nourish themselves. I feel it's important that babies are allowed to indulge their desire to suck.

Some babies are more "sucky" than others; I certainly had one who wanted to suck all the time, whether he was hungry or not. With all four of my sons, I used to put their thumb gently into their mouth so they could suck to soothe themselves. But at the same time, I see nothing wrong with using dummies as comforters, although very young babies will not take to one readily.

While a baby is very young, dummies should be sterilized in exactly the same way as you sterilize feeding bottles and teats (see p. 47). Once your child is being weaned, however, and starts to use his fingers for feeding himself, it is pointless to sterilize dummies. Careful washing and rinsing are all that is needed.

Have several dummies so that they can be changed for fresh ones when they get dirty or damaged. Throw away badly damaged dummies.

SOOTHING YOUR BABY

There are numerous remedies you can try to soothe and console your baby if he's crying. As a general rule, most babies respond to either movement or sound, or both, hence the effectiveness of taking them out in the car, where the motion of the vehicle and the steady humming sound of the engine will usually quieten them. If your baby still seems fretful after your best efforts to soothe him, try some (or all) of the following remedies as part of your repertoire of crying cures (you may find that these movements and sounds relax you as well, which will benefit you both):

• Any movement that rocks him, whether it is you holding and rocking him in your arms, going gently back and forth on a swing, or rocking him in a cradle or rocking chair.
• Walking or dancing with an emphasis on rhythmic movement, since it will remind him of the time when he was being jogged inside your uterus.
• Bouncing him gently in your arms, the cot or on the bed.
• Putting him in a sling (see p. 27) and walking around with him. If you're on your own, just get on with whatever you want to do and try to ignore the crying.
• Taking him for a ride in the car or in a pram, or for a walk in a sling, even at night (you may want to take a mobile phone with you).
• Any form of music as long as it is calm, rhythmic and not too loud; specially recorded sleeping tapes and CDs are available.
• A noisy toy that your baby can shake or rattle.
• A steady household noise, for instance the washing machine.
• Your own soft singing voice, especially if you sing a lullaby.

Bathtime crying
Many young babies cry when they are having a bath, simply because they hate having their skin exposed to the air.

WHAT TO DO WHEN YOUR BABY CRIES

CAUSE OF CRYING	WHAT TO DO
Hunger A hungry cry is nearly always the first cry a parent recognizes and it is the most common reason that young babies cry. They rarely cry after feeding. Babies love the sensation of a full stomach, more than being held or sucking.	Feed on demand. If you have a baby who wants to suck all the time, you don't need to feed; just give him a drink of boiled water. Use a dummy, holding it in his mouth if necessary, so that he can suck on it.
Tiredness Until they're used to their new world, babies cry when they are tired. An observant parent realizes this and will put a baby down.	Lay your baby down where he is quiet and warm. It will also help to wrap or swaddle him before you put him down to sleep.
Lack of contact Some babies will stop crying as soon as you pick them up, because all they want is comfort and a cuddle.	Pick up your baby as soon as he cries. Carry him in a shawl or a sling. Lay him tummy down across your lap and massage his back.
Startling A jerky movement, sudden noise, bright light or rough physical games can upset your baby.	Hold your baby close, rock him gently, and sing to him. Avoid anything that will startle him.
Undressing Most babies dislike undressing: it puts them through unfamiliar movements and they hate the feel of air on their skin.	Undress your baby as little as possible in the first few weeks. When you do, keep up a running commentary of reassuring talk.
Temperature Babies tend to cry if they become too hot or too cold. They may cry if a wet or soiled nappy gets cold or if they are suffering from nappy rash.	Keep your baby's room at 20–22°C (68–72°F). Take off blankets and clothing if he's too hot; add a blanket and another layer of clothing if he's too cold. Change his nappy if necessary.
Pain An ear infection, colic (see right) or other source of pain may cause your baby to cry. If his ear hurts, he may hit it with his fist.	Cuddle your baby and talk soothingly to him. Remove any obvious source of pain, such as a nappy pin. If he seems ill, seek medical advice.

COLIC

Crying caused by colic (a type of abdominal pain) can be distinguished from other forms because it is more of a high-pitched scream than a cry, and usually you'll find that your baby's legs are drawn up to his abdomen and that his face becomes very red.

Colic usually starts in the first three weeks of life and has no known cause. Colicky babies are recognized as quite healthy and continue to thrive.

Colic-related crying usually begins in the early evening between 5 and 6 o'clock, and is seldom pacified by the usual remedies. Colic generally stops of its own accord by the age of three or four months, is rarely serious and needs no treatment; yet parents do find it distressing.

All sorts of causes have been put forward, including wind in the bowel, constipation, over- and underfeeding, and being picked up too much or too little, but tension seems to me the most probable cause. When you're preoccupied with chores, your baby is bound to pick up on the tension and it's quite normal that he should respond with a crying spell.

Since your baby is likely to cry every night for 12 weeks, I'm against using any medicine to forestall the crying. Do try to soothe your baby, but don't expect him to respond readily. Try to remember that the spells come only at night and last for only three months, so there is light at the end of the tunnel.

BE SENSITIVE TO YOUR BABY'S NEEDS

You have to learn to read your baby's signals and gain insight into his needs and desires. Not reading his signals to you, whether they be "I'm hungry", "I'm tired", "I want to be cuddled, not played with", can all result in tears. Once you recognize your baby's cry you have to respond to it, otherwise he's bound to scream even louder and longer. Prolonged crying may make your baby feel very tired, even exhausted, and he will become extremely irritable and difficult to soothe. More importantly, he will quickly learn that pleas for attention go unheeded, and that there's no loving human response when he needs it.

Always be sensitive and alert to your baby's needs. Look, listen, and do your best to interpret what he is trying to say to you through his behaviour; then resolve whatever is causing the alarm immediately. There are all sorts of signs of small discomforts to which you must attend. When your baby has a cold, for instance, his nose may become blocked, making it impossible for him to breathe and feed at the same time, so he'll become angry and frustrated and almost certainly cry.

As you and your baby get to know each other, you will learn to understand what he really wants. If you know, for example, that he's hungry, don't delay his feed by deciding to give him a bath first, simply in order to stick to your routine. Occasionally, you have to ignore routines so that you can respond to your baby's crying.

3

FEEDING
AND
NUTRITION

Infant feeding is about providing adequate nutrition for
your baby. It helps to bear in mind that, while
breastfeeding is certainly best, your baby will still thrive
if you feed her from a bottle. Don't feel guilty or that you
are a bad mother if you make this decision; simply
concentrate on the needs of your baby.

The main things to remember are that you should take
your lead from your baby, and that the love and
affection you give her are as important as any milk.

MILK: THE PERFECT FOOD

In the first few months of her life, your baby will get all the nutrients she requires from breast or formula milk.

Calories *The energy content of food is measured in calories. Infants require around two-and-a-half to three times more calories than adults for their body weight.*

Carbohydrates *These are the principal source of calories.*

Protein *This is essential for building body tissue. A baby's protein requirement is three times as great as an adult's on the basis of body weight.*

Fats *Minute traces of fatty acids are needed for growth and cell repair.*

Breastfeeding
Suckling helps to form a very strong bond between you and your baby from the start.

WHAT YOUR NEWBORN BABY NEEDS

Your baby depends on you for adequate nutrition: breast or bottled milk provides all a newborn needs. Breast milk is her perfect food, but your baby will thrive even if you choose to bottlefeed. Feeding takes a great deal of time, so it's essential to choose a method that suits you both. Well before delivery, you should decide whether you are going to breastfeed or bottlefeed and prepare for whichever you choose.

A baby's nutritional needs reflect her rapid growth in the first months of life: most babies double their birth weight in around four to five months. For healthy development, your baby's food must contain adequate amounts of calories, carbohydrates, protein, fats, vitamins and minerals (see left and far right), and until she's at least four months old, your baby will receive all these nutrients from breast or formula milk. Your baby will cry when she is hungry, so take your lead from her in setting the pattern of feeds.

WHY BREAST IS BEST

Human breast milk doesn't look as rich and creamy as cow's milk, and you may think that it is not good enough for your baby, but don't be put off. It contains all the nutrients in just the right amounts she needs and has many benefits for her. Breastfed babies tend to suffer less than bottlefed babies from illnesses such as chest infections because antibodies from the colostrum (see p. 38) and the breast milk protect the baby. In the first few days of life, these antibodies also protect the intestine, reducing the chance of diarrhoea and vomiting.

Breastfed babies don't get constipated, since breast milk is more easily digested than cow's milk; they are also less prone to ammoniacal nappy rash (see p. 66). From your point of view, breastfeeding is very convenient: you don't need to warm up the milk; there are no bottles to sterilize; no formula has to be made up; and there's no equipment to buy. Breastfed babies usually sleep longer, suffer less from wind, and posset (that is, regurgitate milk) less, and the posset smells less unpleasant. It is difficult to overfeed a breastfed baby, so don't be concerned if your baby seems chubbier than other babies of her age. Each baby has its own appetite and metabolic rate, and yours will be the right weight for her own body.

Some women worry that their breasts will sag if they breast-feed. Your breasts may change in size or sag after the birth, but this comes from being pregnant, not from breastfeeding, which helps you lose weight gained in pregnancy. While you are breastfeeding, the hormone oxytocin (see p. 38), which stimulates milk flow, encourages the uterus to return to its pre-pregnant state; your pelvis and waistline will get back to normal more quickly too. It is also possible that breastfeeding may provide some protection against breast cancer.

THE BENEFITS OF BOTTLEFEEDING

Every woman is capable of breastfeeding her baby, and you should try to do so. Many women think they must breast-feed to be a good mother, and feel guilty if they decide not to. On the other hand, some women find it emotionally or psychologically difficult to breastfeed; others find that they simply cannot master breastfeeding. If this is the case, then you should forget about it and concentrate on giving your baby a good bottlefed diet: she will still thrive. If you decide not to breastfeed at all, your doctor will probably prescribe hormones to suppress your milk supply.

You may consider bottlefeeding because you feel that breastfeeding will tie you down, particularly if you intend to return to work very soon after the birth. This may be the best solution for you, but remember that it is also possible to express enough milk so that your partner or a child-minder can feed your baby while you are away from home. That way, your baby can have all the benefits of your milk, and you can still have the flexibility of bottlefeeding and the freedom that this gives you.

One of the benefits of bottlefeeding is that your partner can be as involved with feeding the new baby as you are. He should try to do this as soon as possible after the birth, so that he can learn to handle the baby confidently and understand her needs. Ideally, he should share the feeding equally with you. Encourage him to hold the baby close and talk or sing to her while feeding, so that she will get used to the feel of his skin, his smell and the sound of his voice.

VITAMIN AND MINERAL NEEDS

As well as the basic nutrients (see far left), milk will supply your baby with necessary vitamins and minerals.

Vitamins These are essential to health. Breast milk does not contain as much vitamin D as formula milks, which contain all the vitamins your baby needs. Ask your health visitor whether your baby requires vitamin supplements.

Minerals Breast and formula milks contain magnesium, calcium and phosphorus, vital for bone and muscle growth. Babies are born with a reserve of iron that will last about four months; after this, they have to be given iron, either in solids or as supplements.

Trace elements Minerals like zinc, copper and fluoride are essential to your baby's health. The first two are present in breast and formula milks, but fluoride, which protects against dental decay, is not. Always check with your midwife or doctor before giving your baby fluoride supplements.

Bottlefeeding
Make feeding a time of closeness and intimacy for you and your new baby.

GOOD MILK SUPPLY

Look after yourself properly by staying relaxed, eating well and drinking enough fluids, and you'll have more than enough milk for your baby.

- *Rest as much as you can, particularly in the first weeks, and try to get plenty of sleep.*

- *You produce most milk in the morning when you are rested. If you become tense during the day, your supply could be poor by evening. Go through your antenatal relaxation routines and have a rest every day.*

- *Let the housework go; do only what is absolutely essential.*

- *Relax with a glass of wine or other treat at the end of the day.*

- *Eat a well-balanced diet that is fairly rich in protein. Avoid highly refined carbohydrates like cakes, biscuits and sweets.*

- *Consult your doctor about taking iron and possibly vitamin supplements.*

- *Drink about three litres of fluid a day. Keep a drink by you while feeding if necessary.*

- *Express any milk your baby doesn't take in the early feeds of the day to encourage your breasts to keep on producing milk.*

- *The combined contraceptive pill decreases your supply: avoid it for five months after delivery. Discuss alternative methods of contraception with your doctor.*

- *Avoid spicy foods, which could affect your milk and upset your baby's stomach.*

ABOUT BREASTFEEDING

Breastfeeding has to be learned, so seek support and advice not just from your midwife or health visitor but from family and friends with babies too. Above all, you will learn from your baby, by understanding and learning how to respond to her signals. Your breasts need no special preparation for feeding, but if you have an inverted nipple, use a breast shell to make it protrude so that your baby can latch on to it. If you are having your baby in hospital, make sure the nursing staff know that you intend to breastfeed, and do not be reticent in asking for help. Suckle your baby from birth (in the delivery room, if you are in hospital) to bond with her as early as possible and to let her get used to suckling.

COLOSTRUM AND BREAST MILK

Water, protein and minerals make up the thin, yellow fluid called colostrum that the breasts produce during the 72 hours after delivery. Colostrum contains antibodies to protect the baby against intestinal and respiratory infections. In the first few days, put your baby regularly to the breast to feed on the colostrum and get used to latching onto the breast (see p. 40).

You may be surprised by the watery appearance of your first milk. When your baby sucks, the first milk that she gets, the foremilk, will be thin, watery and thirst quenching. Then comes the hindmilk, which is richer in fat and protein.

THE LET-DOWN REFLEX

Pituitary gland

Hypothalamus

How the let-down reflex works
When your baby sucks at the breast, the sucking action sends messages to the hypothalamus, which in turn stimulates the pituitary gland in your brain to release two hormones: prolactin, which stimulates the milk glands to produce milk; and oxytocin, which causes milk to be passed from the glands to the milk reservoirs behind the areola. This transfer is commonly known as the let-down reflex.

RELAXED POSITIONS FOR BREASTFEEDING

Lying down is ideal for night feeds; when your baby is still very small, you may need to lay her on a pillow so that she can reach your nipple. You may find a lying position best after an episiotomy if sitting is uncomfortable. If you've had a Caesarean section, try lying with your baby's legs tucked under your arm.

Make sure you are both comfortable

Lying positions
Breastfeeding positions in which you can lie down are a restful alternative to sitting ones and will keep a wriggling baby off a tender Caesarean incision.

Sitting position
Make sure that your arms and back are supported and you feel comfortably relaxed.

Nursing bras
Always wear a supportive nursing bra that has front fastenings and wide straps; try it on before you buy it. Drop-front or zip-fastening bras are easy to undo with one hand while you hold your baby. A good bra will minimize discomfort if your breasts become sore.

SUPPLY AND DEMAND

Milk is produced in glands that are buried deep in the breast, not in its fatty tissue, so breast size is no indication of how much milk you can produce; even small breasts give a perfectly good supply.

Milk is produced according to demand: you supply what your baby needs, so don't worry that you'll run out of milk if she feeds very often. Your baby's sucking stimulates your breasts to produce milk, so the more eagerly she feeds, the more milk they will produce – and vice versa. During the time you are breastfeeding, the amount of milk available will fluctuate according to your baby's needs. Once she becomes established on solids, your breasts will naturally produce less milk.

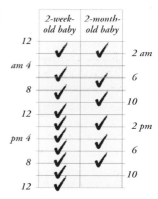

	2-week-old baby	2-month-old baby	
12	✓	✓	2 am
am 4	✓	✓	6
8	✓	✓	10
12	✓	✓	2 pm
pm 4	✓	✓	6
8	✓	✓	10
12	✓		

How often will she feed?
At first, your baby will feed little and often. By about two months, she will be feeding roughly every four hours and will take more at each feed than she did in earlier days.

HOW LONG ON EACH BREAST?

You should keep your baby on the breast for as long as she shows interest in sucking.

• *If your baby continues to suck after your breasts have been emptied, she may just be enjoying it. This is fine if it's not making your nipples sore.*

• *Gently take your baby off your nipple (see below right) when she has finished feeding from one breast and put her on the other. She may not suck for so long on the second breast.*

• *Alternate the first breast you offer at each feed. Put a safety pin on your bra to remind you which breast was last suckled.*

Latching on
Your baby should take the nipple and a good part of the areola into her mouth. Milk is drawn out by sucking, and by squeezing the nipple against the roof of her mouth.

BREASTFEEDING YOUR BABY

When feeding time is both relaxed and pleasurable, breast-feeding creates a strong bond between mother and baby. Make sure your baby can see you, and smile and talk to her while she is suckling. She will soon come to associate the pleasure of feeding with the sight of your face, the sound of your voice and the smell of your skin. Make sure you are both comfortable before you start (see p. 39). You should feed your baby from both breasts, and you may like to wind her before changing over (see p. 51).

RECOGNIZING COMMON PROBLEMS

It is perfectly normal for breastfeeding not to go smoothly at first, so try not to get worked up or anxious about minor setbacks such as your baby refusing a feed. Remember that she too is learning and that it will take time for you to get used to each other, so persevere, and consult your midwife or health visitor for suggestions and helpful advice.

Refusing the breast It is entirely usual for a newborn not to suck very vigorously or for very long during her first 24 to 36 hours. If this happens later, however, there may be a problem that needs dealing with. Breathing difficulties are the most likely reason for a baby to be having problems taking the breast. It may be that your breast is covering her

BREASTFEEDING

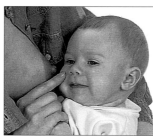

The rooting reflex
Prompt your baby to look for your breast by gently stroking the cheek nearest to it. Your baby will turn at once towards your breast, open mouthed.

Releasing the nipple
To break the suction, slip your little finger into the corner of the baby's mouth. Your breast will slip out easily instead of being dragged out.

nostrils; if so, gently pull the breast back and away from the baby's face, just above the areola. If her nose seems to be snuffly or blocked, consult your doctor, who will probably prescribe nose drops to clear the nostrils.

If there's no obvious cause for your baby's refusal to feed, she may simply be fretful. A baby who has been crying with hunger or has been changed, fussed over or played with when she's hungry can become too distressed to take the breast. You'll need to soothe her by holding her firmly and talking or singing to her; there will be little point in trying to feed her until she's calmed down.

If there has been some delay in starting to breastfeed (as with a premature baby who has had to be bottlefed), your baby may find it more difficult to take the breast, and you will have to be patient and persevering. Your midwife or health visitor will advise you if you need to give expressed milk from a special cup until the baby can take all she needs from the breast. Supplementary bottles (see p. 43) are rarely necessary, and may cause mothers to give up breastfeeding. Giving your own expressed milk is a better alternative.

Comfort sucking The majority of babies enjoy sucking on their mothers' breasts for its own sake just as much as for feeding. You will learn to tell the difference between actual feeding and comfort sucking. During a feed, you may notice that your baby is sucking strongly but without swallowing. Provided your nipples are not sore, there is no reason why your baby shouldn't suck for as long as she wants, although she takes most of her feed in the first 3–5 minutes.

Sleeping through feeds If your baby seems to have little interest in food during the first few days, make sure that she takes as much as she wants from one breast. If she sleeps at the breast, it means that she is contented and doing well, although premature babies, who tend to sleep a lot, need to be woken and fed regularly. If your baby does fall asleep at the breast, wake her gently half an hour later and offer a feed; if she is hungry, she will perk up.

Fretful feeding If your baby doesn't settle down to feed, or appears not to be satisfied, she is probably just sucking on the nipple and not getting enough milk. This may also lead to sore nipples. Check that your baby is properly latched on, and has a good proportion of the areola in her mouth.

UNDERFEEDING

It is rare for a breastfed baby not to get enough milk, even if you cannot see how much she has taken.

• *Continuing to suck even after she has finished feeding from both breasts may signify enjoyment rather than hunger.*

• *Thirst may make your baby go on sucking after emptying your breasts. Try giving about 30 ml (1 fl oz) of cooled, boiled water from a bottle, feeding cup or baby beaker.*

• *If your baby seems fretful and hungry, have her weighed at your clinic to check if she is gaining weight as quickly as expected. If not, your milk supply has been reduced, perhaps because you are tired or run down. Supplementary feeds (see p. 43) from a special cup may be the answer until your supply is back to normal. Consult your doctor if you are at all worried.*

• *Low-milk syndrome (a rare condition in which a newborn fails to get enough nutrition) is nearly always due to the baby's difficulties in learning how to latch on and suckle. In a very few cases, the mother may just not be producing enough milk. You can continue breastfeeding, but supplementary bottles will be needed. I cannot say too often that mothers and babies must be given time to get the hang of breastfeeding.*

• *If your baby wets fewer than six nappies a day, check with your midwife or doctor. It may be a warning of dehydration.*

EXPRESSING TIPS

Make expressing milk as easy on yourself as possible, and take care to store it correctly.

• *Leaning over a low surface while expressing may give you backache. Have the container at a convenient height.*

• *Expressing milk should be entirely painless. If it hurts, stop at once. Ask your midwife or health visitor if you are doing it correctly.*

• *The more relaxed you are, the easier it will be to express. If the milk won't start to flow, place a warm flannel over your breasts to open the ducts, or try expressing while in the bath.*

• *If you're concerned that your baby might not go back to breastfeeding after getting used to the bottle's teat, try feeding her milk from a specially designed cup, or spooning the expressed milk from a cup. Make sure that both spoon and cup are sterilized before use.*

• *Your hands must be clean, and every piece of equipment and all containers that you are using should be sterile.*

• *Breast milk will go off if it is incorrectly stored, and could make your baby ill. Refrigerate or freeze your milk as soon as you've collected it. Refrigerated milk keeps for 24 hours, frozen for up to six months.*

• *Expressed milk should be put into sterile, sealable containers. Don't use glass containers if you want to freeze your milk: they might crack. Use sterile plastic bottle liners instead.*

EXPRESSING MILK

You can store expressed milk in the refrigerator or freezer. This will free you from feeling tied down by breastfeeding, allow your baby to be fed with your milk if you're away, and give your partner the chance to share in the feeding.

Express milk by hand or with a manual or electric breast pump; hand expressing may be easiest and most convenient. Before starting, you will need a bowl, funnel and container that can be sealed. Sterilize all the equipment in a sterilizing solution, or with boiling water or in a special steam unit.

In the first six weeks, hand expressing is nearly always a bit difficult, as the breasts have not reached full production, but don't give up. Because breasts produce milk in response to demand, you may need to express milk in order to keep your supply going – if your baby is premature and can't yet breastfeed, for instance. Even if you use a pump, it is worth learning the technique of hand expressing in case you need it. The best time for expressing is in the morning, when you'll have the most milk, although when your baby drops the night feed, you may find evening a better time.

EXPRESSING BY PUMP

All manual pumps work by means of suction and come in three parts: a funnel or shield, the pump mechanism, and a container. Assembling and operating the pump will vary a little between brands. Simply follow the manufacturer's instructions.

Pump mechanism

Funnel

Container doubles as feeding bottle

Using a manual pump
Place the shield over your nipple and then squeeze and release the handle. Your milk should be drawn into the vacuum created in the bottle. If this causes you any pain, stop at once: expressing milk should be painless. Relax and try again a little later.

EXPRESSING BY HAND

Massaging the outer breast
Wash your hands. Cup your breast in both hands with the fingers underneath and the thumbs above. Squeeze the outer part of your breast gently and firmly between your fingers and thumbs. Repeat ten times, moving around the breast as you do so.

Massaging the inner breast
Move your hands closer to the areola and then repeat the squeezing procedure as above.

Massaging the breast stimulates milk flow

Press back gently and rhythmically

Express from each breast alternately

Starting the flow
Place the thumb and fingers of one hand near the areola, press them back into your ribs, then squeeze gently and rhythmically. If the milk doesn't begin to flow immediately, keep on trying.

SUPPLEMENTARY BOTTLES

Even if you are breastfeeding, occasions may arise when you have to give supplementary bottles of formula milk.

If you have a particularly sore nipple or a blocked duct (see pp. 44 and 45), you may wish to give supplementary bottles, although many mothers express milk from the affected breast and use this in the bottle.

A baby who has become used to the nipple may dislike plastic teats. It can be difficult to tell, unfortunately, whether your baby just dislikes the teat or is not hungry. If you persist, she'll eventually get used to the bottle, but you may then find that she doesn't want to go back to the breast. If this happens, try giving the milk from a sterilized spoon or cup.

Relief bottles containing your own expressed milk can be given to your baby if you are unable to breastfeed or if you are leaving the baby with someone else.

Emptying the breast
Continue to work on the breast for about five minutes, moving around the areola, then go on to the second breast. Repeat the whole procedure for both breasts.

Make sure the container is at a convenient height for you

HELP FOR SORE NIPPLES

Suckling your baby can cause soreness around the nipples, especially if your skin is fair. The following tips may help to minimize any problems.

- *Always make sure that your baby has the nipple and areola well into her mouth.*

- *Always take your baby off the breast gently (see p. 40).*

- *Keep your nipples as dry as possible between feeds.*

- *Make sure your nipples are dry before putting your bra back on after a feed.*

- *Wear disposable, washable pads or clean handkerchiefs inside your bra to soak up leaking milk.*

- *If you are feeding from one breast only, use a breast shell to collect excess milk that drips or flows from the other. Store the milk in the refrigerator for 24 hours; or you can freeze it.*

- *If one of your nipples does become sore, give that breast a rest from feeding and comfort sucks for 24 hours, or until the soreness has gone. Express milk from the affected breast and feed from the other one.*

- *Wear a soft silicone shield. This fits over the nipple and the baby sucks through a small teat on the front. Sterilize the shield each time before using.*

- *A sore nipple may become cracked. To prevent this, gently apply a soothing chamomile or calendula cream two or three times every day.*

MANAGING BREASTFEEDING

Breastfeeding may go smoothly right from the start, but it is also normal for you to be a bit clumsy at first, for the baby not to suck for very long, or for your breasts to be a bit sore. Learning takes time, so persevere until things get easier.

CARE OF THE BREASTS

Keeping your breasts and nipples clean is very important. You need to cleanse them every day with water or baby lotion (not soap, which defats the skin and can aggravate a sore or cracked nipple) and gently pat them dry. Dry them gently after feeding. Wear your bra all the time, as you will need its support; but leave the front flaps down with your nipples open to the air whenever you can. Consider using a moisturizing cream on your nipples. If they become sore, try chamomile or calendula cream or an antiseptic spray.

Once your milk flow is established, the milk may leak out quite a lot. Use breast pads, handkerchiefs or a plastic breast shell (see left) to soak up or catch leaks. Change pads and handkerchiefs often, and sterilize the shell before re-using.

WHAT HAPPENS IF YOU ARE ILL

If you are confined to bed, you can express milk so that your partner can feed the baby when you are not feeling up to it. If you are too ill even to express your milk, then your baby can be given formula milk by bottle or by spoon and, although she may not like this at first, she will take the milk as she becomes more and more hungry.

You can still breastfeed if you have to go into hospital. Inform the nursing staff as soon as possible that this is what you intend to do so they have time to make the necessary arrangements: for instance, someone will have to be on hand to lift and change your baby if you are too tired or ill to do so. If you have an operation, however, you will not be able to breastfeed afterwards because of the anaesthetic – you'll be too groggy and, more importantly, the drugs you have been given will have passed into your milk. If you know you'll be having an operation, try to express and freeze milk so that your baby can be bottlefed until you have recovered. It will take up to ten days for your milk to return: let your baby comfort suck as often as she wishes, meanwhile.

WHAT TO DO IF PROBLEMS ARISE

Your breasts will be working hard for the next few months, and problems may arise if, for instance, your baby is not latching on properly or drags on the nipple as she comes off (see p. 40). Keep your breasts clean and dry, make sure your baby empties them when she feeds, wear a proper nursing bra and act at once if your nipples get sore or cracked.

Cracked nipple Not dealt with properly, sore nipples (see far left) may become cracked: you'll feel a shooting pain as your baby suckles. Keep the nipple dry with breast pads or clean tissues and stop feeding from the affected breast until it has healed. Instead, feed hand-expressed milk to your baby by bottle or from a baby beaker (sterilize both before using).

Engorgement Towards the end of the first week of breast-feeding (before it is properly established), your breasts may become over full and painful and quite hard to the touch; your baby won't be able to latch on successfully. Make sure you wear a good nursing bra to minimize discomfort and gently express some milk (see pp. 42 and 43) before feeding to relieve the fullness. Having warm baths will also help to relieve the discomfort by encouraging your milk to flow.

Blocked duct Tight clothing or engorgement can cause a milk duct to become blocked, resulting in a hard red patch on the outside of the breast where the duct lies. Prevent this by feeding often and encouraging your baby to empty your breasts; check that your bra fits properly too. If you do get a blocked duct, feed often and offer the affected breast first.

Mastitis A blocked duct that is not treated can lead to an acute infection: mastitis. The breast will be inflamed and a red patch will appear on the outside, as with a blocked duct. You need to empty the breast, so go on breastfeeding. Your doctor may prescribe antibiotics to clear up the infection.

Breast abscess An untreated blocked duct or mastitis can result in a breast abscess. You may feel feverish and have an exquisitely tender, shiny red patch on your breast. If treatment with antibiotics fails, the abscess needs to be drained surgically, but you may be able to go on breastfeeding even if you need this minor operation – ask your doctor's advice.

THE PILL AND BREASTFEEDING

If you can, avoid all drugs when you are breastfeeding. Many medications pass from your body into the breast milk and can affect your baby.

● *If you want to breastfeed and use oral contraceptives, take the progestogen-only "mini-pill": the oestrogen in the combined pill may reduce your milk supply.*

● *How progestogen affects the baby is not yet fully known, so it is best to use some other form of contraception until your baby has been weaned.*

● *Ask your doctor or family planning clinic for advice in helping you choose the method of contraception that is best and most suitable for you.*

● *If you are already taking medications or consult your doctor about new problems, always inform her that you are breastfeeding.*

MILK FORMULAS

A variety of milk formulas is available, all with carefully balanced ingredients to make them as close as possible to breast milk; in fact, formula milk has added vitamin D and iron, levels of which are quite low in breast milk.

Most formulas are based on cow's milk, but you can buy soya-based formulas if cow's milk is unsuitable for your baby. Some formulas come both in powder and ready-mixed forms.

Ready-mixed milk in cartons or ready-to-feed bottles is ultra-heat treated (UHT), which means it is sterile and will keep in a cool place until the "best before" or "sell by" date. Once the carton has been opened, the milk will keep for 24 hours in the refrigerator. Ready-mixed milk is more expensive than powdered formula, but it is very convenient, and you may like to use it when travelling.

If you use powdered formula, it's essential that you make it up precisely according to the manufacturer's instructions. Some parents are tempted to add extra powder to make the milk "more nourishing". If you do this, your baby will just be getting too much protein and fat, and not enough water.

If you add too little powder, your baby will not be getting the nutrients she needs for healthy growth.

BOTTLES AND MILK

Most babies end up being bottlefed at some stage (if not continuously right from the start, then often after weaning or with supplementary bottles): all of them thrive. New infant formulas, bottles and teats come onto the market regularly, all with the aim of making bottlefeeding as convenient and as similar to breastfeeding as possible.

The one important thing you cannot give your baby if you bottlefeed from birth is colostrum (see p. 38), so even if you're not intending to continue breastfeeding your baby, you'll be giving her the best possible start if you put her to the breast in the first few days. If you decide not to do this (or for some reason cannot), the hospital staff will take care of your baby's first feeds; she will probably be given glucose water a few hours after delivery.

One of the advantages of bottlefeeding is that the new father can be just as involved as the new mother at feeding times. Make sure that your partner feeds your baby as soon as possible after the birth. This way, he can get used to the technique, won't be worried about handling her and can learn to do all the things your baby needs. He should have his chest bare so that the baby can nestle up to his skin when she feeds, and bond with his smell.

STERILIZING THE BOTTLES

It is a good idea to practise with your feeding equipment before you go into hospital, so buy it well in advance of your delivery date. Large department stores and pharmacies sell bottlefeeding packs that have all the essential equipment.

BOTTLES AND TEATS

Bottles (left to right)
Tapered bottle
Waisted bottle
Easy-grip bottle
Disposable bottle; liners

Teats (left to right)
Universal latex teats (2)
Silicone anti-colic teat
Natural-shaped teat
Wide-based teat for
    disposable bottle

CLEANING BOTTLES AND TEATS

A bottle brush helps remove all traces of milk

Use salt to remove any milk trapped in the teat

Cleaning the bottles
Use a bottle brush and warm solution of washing-up liquid to remove all traces of milk from the bottles. Rinse well.

Cleaning the teats
Rinse the teats thoroughly. Remove all traces of milk by rubbing them with fine salt, then rinse again thoroughly.

Keep your sterilizing equipment in the kitchen, preferably near the sink. To use the cold-water sterilizing method with sterilizing tablets, fill the unit with cold water up to the guide mark, then dissolve one or two tablets in the water, according to the manufacturer's instructions. Clean the bottles and teats as described above, then put them with the measuring jug, spoon and knife into the unit, making sure that all the equipment is submerged (fill the bottles with water so that they stay under the sterilizing solution and don't bob about). Leave the equipment for the required time, and rinse and drain when you are ready to use it.

The majority of sterilizing units usually hold only four to six bottles. Your newborn baby, however, will be taking something like seven feeds over 24 hours, so you may have to sterilize and prepare the bottles twice a day – morning and evening – to make sure that you have enough feed ready and waiting for whenever she is hungry. As your baby grows, the number of feeds will decline, so you'll be able to make up all the feeds she needs in a single batch.

You will soon develop your own routine, but I always found it most convenient to sterilize and make up a full batch of bottles (see p. 48) and then refrigerate them until needed. After the feed, rinse the bottle in warm water and put it aside. It is wise to continue sterilizing all milk-feeding equipment until your baby is nine months old.

STERILIZING METHODS

Cold-water sterilization and boiling are both effective methods. It is as well to be aware of other methods in case you're away from home, or run out of tablets to use in a sterilizing unit.

• *Put all the equipment into a large, covered, plastic container and use sterilizing tablets (or fluid) and cold water.*

• *Steam sterilizing units quickly and effectively destroy bacteria on your equipment.*

• *You can sterilize the feeding equipment in a microwave, using a specially designed steam unit, as long as the equipment is suitable for microwave use.*

• *A simple sterilizing method is to wash the equipment and boil it for at least 25 minutes in a large, covered pan.*

• *You can wash the feeding bottles, jug and knife on a normal dishwasher cycle; but put the teats in a covered pan and boil them separately.*

Using a ready-made formula is more straightforward than mixing your own – but you still need to observe strict rules of hygiene.

● *Before opening the carton, use a clean brush to scrub its top. Pay particular attention to the cutting line.*

● *Use clean scissors to cut the corner off the carton. Avoid touching the cut edges, as you could contaminate the milk.*

● *If you are not using all of the milk, leave the excess in the carton; it can be stored in the refrigerator for 24 hours.*

● *Throw away milk left in the bottle after a feed; saliva will have contaminated it.*

MILK FLOW

The hole in the teat should be large enough to let the milk flow in a stream of several drops per second when the bottle is inverted.

Too large a hole means your baby will get too much too fast and splutter; too small, and she will get tired before she is satisfied. You can buy teats with holes of different sizes that allow the milk to flow faster or slower. Make sure you buy the correct size for your baby's needs.

Choose sculpted teats for preference. They are shaped to fit the baby's palate and allow her control over the flow.

BOTTLEFEEDING YOUR BABY

Before you start giving your baby a bottle feed, you need to bear in mind a couple of essential points. The formula must be properly made up, using the specified quantities, so that your baby gets the correct balance of both nutrients and water; and when feeding, your baby should be able to draw milk at a rate that is comfortable for her. You can make up one bottle at a time, mixing it in the bottle according to the manufacturer's instructions, or a batch of several.

MAKING UP A BATCH OF FORMULA

Equipment
Bottles and lids; plastic knife; measuring scoop from formula pack; funnel; teats; caps and jug. Rinse with boiled water and drain before use.

Level off powder w back of kn

Measuring
Use the scoop that comes with the formula to measure out the required amount. Level each scoopful with a knife; do not pack the formula into the scoop.

A sterilized funnel may be helpful

Mixing
Put the required amount of formula into the mixing jug with the boiled and cooled water. Never be tempted to add extra formula; this will make the formula too concentrated and could be dangerous. Stir the formula and water until you are sure that there are no lumps or residue left and that the mixture is completely smooth.

Storing
Place the sterilized teats upside down in the bottles. Secure them with the screw-on lids and put on the plastic caps. Refrigerate the bottles as soon as they are made; you may need to put them on a tray to keep them upright.

GIVING A BOTTLE FEED

Make yourself comfortable, with your arms well supported. Hold your baby half-sitting with her head in the crook of your elbow and her back along your forearm; this will allow her to swallow safely and easily. Keep your face close to hers and chat to her all the time. Or you may like to try other positions (see p. 39) until you discover which one suits you both best. Lying down with your baby tucked under your arm is especially comfortable for night feeds.

Before you begin feeding, test the heat of the milk; you should already have tested the flow (see far left). If your baby is having difficulty drawing the milk, gently remove the bottle from her mouth so that air can enter the bottle, then continue as before. Hold the bottle at a slight angle so that the milk covers the teat completely and your baby does not swallow air with the milk as she sucks.

BOTTLEFEEDING

Giving the bottle
Gently stroke your baby's nearest cheek to elicit her sucking reflex. Insert the teat carefully into her mouth. If you push the teat too far back in, she may gag on it.

Make feeding times pleasant
Chat to your baby and smile at her while feeding. Let her pause mid-feed if she likes, changing her onto the other arm to give her a new view and your arm a rest.

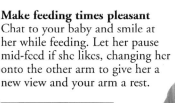

Removing the bottle
Gently slide your little finger into the corner of her mouth to break the suction on the teat.

WARMING THE BOTTLE

Some mothers like to warm the bottle, although the milk will be perfectly all right if it has just been brought to room temperature. Don't warm the bottle in a microwave: they do not always heat evenly, and may create "hot spots" in the milk that could scald your baby's mouth.

Warming the milk
Place the bottle in a bowl of hot water for a few minutes. You could also run it under the hot tap, shaking it all the time.

Testing milk temperature
Try a few drops on your wrist; it should feel neither hot nor cold to the touch.

BOTTLEFEEDING ROUTINES

Bottlefed babies tend to be fed less frequently than breastfed ones. This is because formula milk takes longer to digest and contains slightly more protein, and therefore satisfies hunger for longer. A four-hourly regime of six feeds a day seems to suit most bottlefed babies after the first two or three days, whereas breastfed babies will probably take seven feeds a day. When first born, your baby is unlikely to take much over 60 millilitres (2 fluid ounces) at each feed, but as she grows she will take fewer and larger feeds.

Never feed your baby according to the clock: allow her to determine when she is to be fed. She will let you know quite clearly with cries when she is hungry. Your baby's appetite will vary, so if she seems satisfied, let her leave what she does not want. Don't feel that your baby has to finish the bottle at each feed. She will only get overfull and posset it back (see p. 52) or – worse – become overfed and fat. On the other hand, if your baby is still hungry, give her some extra from another bottle. If this happens regularly, start to make more milk for every feed.

NIGHT FEEDS

Your baby will need feeding at least once during the night, and this break in your sleep on top of all the other things that you have to do to take care of her may make you extremely tired and tense. The problem is not so much the number of hours' sleep that you lose, but more the way in which your sleep patterns are broken over long periods. For this reason, it is very important that you get adequate rest, day and night, and, as you are doing most of the feeding, try to get your partner to take on some of the other jobs.

REDUCING NIGHT FEEDS

At first, three hours is the longest time your baby will be able to sleep without being woken by hunger. Once she reaches a weight of around 5 kilograms (11 pounds), try to stretch the time between feeds with the aim of making sure that you are getting about six hours of undisturbed sleep at night. Although your baby will have her own routine, it's sensible to try to time her last feed to coincide with your own bedtime, which should be as late as possible. You may find that your baby will still wake up and demand the early morning feed, no matter how much you try to change her routine. If this happens, you'll just have to be patient, make the night feeds as comfortable as possible, and look forward to when she drops the early morning feed.

OVERFEEDING

Chubby babies can look cuddly and attractive, but fat cells, once produced, can't be removed, and a fat baby may grow into a fat adult, with all the attendant risks to health. Sadly, it is easy to overfeed a bottlefed baby. The reasons for this are twofold: first, it is tempting to put extra formula into the bottle, but you should always follow the instructions precisely (see p. 48), otherwise you'll be giving the baby calories that are not needed. Second, in your anxiety to feed her "properly", you'll want to see your baby finish the last drop of her feed, but you should always let her decide when she has finished. Giving sweet, syrupy drinks and introducing solids too early can also cause overfeeding.

UNDERFEEDING

It is rare for bottlefed babies to be underfed. You should feed your baby on demand and not at set times, and you will find that demands vary from day to day. If you insist on feeding to a schedule, never giving extra milk and refusing interim feeds even when your baby is crying for them, then she won't get all the milk that she needs.

If your baby seems fretful time and again after she drains each bottle, she may well be hungry. In this case, offer her an extra 60 millilitres (2 fluid ounces) of formula. If she takes it, then she needs it.

If your baby demands frequent feeds but doesn't take much, the teat hole may be too small (see p. 48), so that she is having difficulty sucking the milk and becomes tired with sucking before she gets enough.

WINDING

Winding releases any air that your baby may have swallowed during feeding or in crying prior to feeding. Babies vary greatly in their reaction to wind and it's unlikely to cause discomfort; many babies are not noticeably happier or more contented for

HYGIENE AND PREPARATION

Your baby needs protecting from bacteria, so make sure that all feeding equipment is scrupulously clean, and take care with the storage and preparation of formula.

- *Read and follow sterilizing instructions carefully.*

- *Wash your hands before you sterilize equipment, prepare bottles or give feeds.*

- *Never add extra formula; follow the instructions closely.*

- *Give the milk to your baby as soon as it has been warmed up.*

- *When making batches, cool the formula as soon as it is ready. Don't store warm milk in a vacuum flask where germs will breed.*

- *Refrigerate prepared bottles until needed.*

- *Keep opened packets of ready-mixed formula in the refrigerator.*

- *Throw away milk left over after a feed.*

How to wind
Hold your baby close to you. Gently but firmly stroke or pat her back to help her bring up any bubbles of air.

having been winded. Swallowing air is more common in bottlefed babies, but you can prevent it to some extent by tilting the bottle more as your baby empties it, so that the teat is full of milk and not air, or by using disposable bottles. The one real point in favour of winding your baby, whether you are breast- or bottlefeeding, is that it makes you pause, relax, slow down, hold your baby gently and stroke or pat her reassuringly, and this is good for both of you. Therefore, the way I look at winding is this: by all means do it, if only for your own peace of mind, but don't become fanatical about it.

POSSETTING

If your baby tends to posset, that is, regurgitate milk (some babies never do), you may wonder if she's keeping enough down. My youngest son was a child who tended to posset, and I worried in case he wasn't getting enough to eat. I simply followed my own instinct, which was to offer him more food. When he didn't take it, I assumed that he had possetted an excess that he didn't need. The commonest cause of possetting in very young babies is overfeeding, and this is another reason why you should never insist that your bottlefed baby finishes her feed.

Forcible vomiting – where the milk is projected out of the baby's mouth with force – should be reported right away to your doctor, especially if it occurs consistently after several feeds. Vomiting in a small baby is always very serious since it can quickly lead to dehydration, and you should seek medical advice as soon as possible.

4

BATHING, CHANGING AND DRESSING

Your role in your baby's everyday care is to keep him
strong and healthy not just by meeting his dietary needs,
but by looking after his hygiene and physical comfort.
Keeping your baby clean will at first involve what seems
like an endless round of changing nappies; but don't
despair, for this stage does eventually pass.
Most mothers enjoy choosing baby clothes, and while
you might like to buy some dressy outfits for
special occasions, you need not spend a lot of money.

WASHING A GIRL

There is no need to open the lips of your baby girl's vulva to clean inside; indeed, you should never try to do so. Just wash the skin of the nappy area and dry it carefully.

When washing your baby girl, take care to wipe from front to back (in other words, towards the anus) when you clean the nappy area. This will avoid soiling the vulva and minimize the risk of spreading bacteria from the bowels to the bladder, which could cause infection.

BATHING AND HYGIENE

Part of your daily routine will be to keep your baby clean. Many new parents worry about handling a very small baby in the baby bath, but you will soon get used to bathtimes and look forward to it as an opportunity to have fun and play with your baby. Instead of feeling apprehensive, set aside half an hour, have everything you need around you, try to relax and you will enjoy it.

A young baby doesn't need bathing very often because only his bottom, face and neck, and skin creases get dirty, so you need to bathe him only every two or three days; in between times, you can just top and tail him (see below). This allows you to attend to the parts of your baby that really need washing with as little disturbance and distress to him as possible. You should use cooled, boiled water for a newborn, but when your baby is a little older (at about one month), you can use warm water straight from the tap. Do wash your baby's hair often to prevent cradle cap from forming (see p. 57); the act of washing removes any scales. You needn't use soap for a newborn; from about six weeks, bath lotion, soap or other baby toiletries are fine.

Babies don't like having their skin exposed to the air, so while you are washing your baby, keep him undressed for the minimum time necessary. Warm a big, fluffy towel on a not-too-hot radiator and have it ready to hand to wrap your baby in as soon as you are finished.

TOPPING AND TAILING YOUR BABY

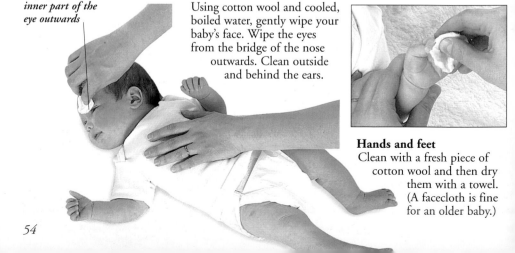

Wipe from the inner part of the eye outwards

Face and ears
Using cotton wool and cooled, boiled water, gently wipe your baby's face. Wipe the eyes from the bridge of the nose outwards. Clean outside and behind the ears.

Hands and feet
Clean with a fresh piece of cotton wool and then dry them with a towel. (A facecloth is fine for an older baby.)

BODY CARE

Once you have taken care of your baby's nappy area and made sure that his skin is kept free from any traces of food or dirt that might cause irritation, the rest will take care of itself.

Eyes, nose and ears Wash your baby's eyes with balls of cotton wool and some cooled, boiled water. Work from the inner part of the eye to the outer, using a fresh piece of cotton wool for each eye to avoid spreading any infection.

Don't poke around inside your baby's nose and ears; they are self-cleaning, so don't use nose or ear drops except on your doctor's advice. Just clean his ears with moist cotton wool. If you see wax in your baby's ears, don't try to scrape it out. It is a natural secretion of the canal of the outer ear, is antiseptic and protects the eardrum from dust and grit. Removing it will simply cause the ear to produce more wax. If you are concerned, consult your doctor.

Nails Keep your newborn baby's nails short so he does not scratch his skin. Cut them after a bath, when they are soft, using small, blunt-ended scissors; or bite the nails off with your teeth. Your mouth is so sensitive, you won't hurt him.

Navel During the few days after birth, the umbilical stump dries, shrivels and drops off (see p. 13). You can bathe your baby before the stump has healed, but do dry it thoroughly afterwards. Allow the area to stay open to the air as much as possible to help speed up the shrinking and healing process.

WASHING A BOY

Never pull back your baby boy's foreskin for cleaning; it's quite tight and could get stuck (by the time he is three or four, the foreskin will be loose and can retract without force). Wash the whole of the nappy area and dry carefully, particularly the skin creases.

If your baby has just been circumcised, watch carefully for any signs of bleeding. You may expect to see a few drops of blood: this is normal. Slight inflammation and swelling are also normal, and these will settle down in a short while.

If bleeding persists, however, or if there is any sign of infection, consult your doctor. Make sure to get advice about bathing your baby and particular care of the penis, and what to do about the dressing if one has been applied.

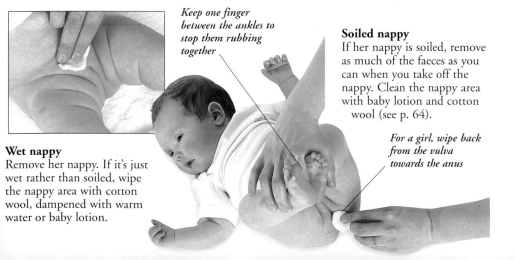

Wet nappy
Remove her nappy. If it's just wet rather than soiled, wipe the nappy area with cotton wool, dampened with warm water or baby lotion.

Keep one finger between the ankles to stop them rubbing together

Soiled nappy
If her nappy is soiled, remove as much of the faeces as you can when you take off the nappy. Clean the nappy area with baby lotion and cotton wool (see p. 64).

For a girl, wipe back from the vulva towards the anus

TOILETRIES

A newborn's skin is delicate. You should not use soap or wipes until your baby is at least six weeks old; it will remove the natural oils from his skin and leave it dry and uncomfortable. Special baby toiletries are mild and will not irritate your baby's skin; many are hypoallergenic too.

• *A little baby oil in your baby's bath water is a good moisturizer for very dry skin.*

• *For delicate skin, like the nappy area, baby lotion is an ideal cleanser and moisturizer.*

• *Baby powder can be drying to your baby's skin. If you use it, shake it onto your hand first, or your baby may inhale it. Never use powder on the skin creases, where it can cake and cause irritation.*

• *Zinc and castor oil cream or petroleum jelly are waterproof and will protect your baby's skin from urine. Medicated nappy creams containing titanium salts are good if your baby has nappy rash (see p. 67).*

Use cotton wool and baby lotion to clean your baby's nappy area

GIVING A SPONGE BATH

If your baby really hates being undressed, or if you are a bit daunted by giving him a bath, a sponge bath is the answer. Hold your baby securely on your lap while removing the least amount of clothing at any time. If you find it hard to manoeuvre your baby while he is on your lap, put him on a changing mat and follow the same sponge bath method, taking care to keep one half covered while washing the other. Put a bowl of warm water near you before you begin.

SPONGE BATH

Upper body
Sit your baby on a towel on your lap. Undress the top half of his body and wash his front with a sponge or cloth. Pat him dry. Lean him forward over your arm and wash his back.

Nappy area or hair wash
Either wash your baby's hair (see right) at this stage, or dress his top half in clean clothes and remove his lower clothing and nappy. Clean the nappy area (see p. 64).

Lower body
Use the sponge or cloth to wash his legs and feet. Pat dry, put on barrier cream (if you use it) and a clean nappy and dress him.

HAIR CARE AND WASHING

From birth, wash your baby's hair daily, but don't feel you have to use shampoo: bath lotion dissolved in water will do. After about 12–16 weeks, wash his hair with water daily and once or twice a week with baby shampoo. Choose a non-sting variety, but do still take care to avoid getting it near his eyes. For a small baby, you can tuck his legs under your armpit while supporting the back and cradling the head (see p. 58); or sit on the edge of the bath with the baby across your legs, facing you, to make him feel secure if he's scared of water. Don't be nervous about the fontanelles (see p. 12); the membrane covering them is very tough, and there is no need to scrub the hair, so you can do no harm if you are gentle.

Apply the shampoo or bath lotion to your baby's hair and gradually work it in until a lather forms. Wait for about 15 seconds before rinsing it off; there is no need to apply it a second time. To rinse the hair, just use a flannel dipped in warm water to wipe away the suds; do your best to remove every trace of soap. When drying your baby's hair, try not to cover his face or he may panic and start to cry. It is best just to use the end of the towel to avoid this.

IF YOUR BABY DISLIKES HAIR WASHING…

Many babies hate having their hair washed, even if they enjoy having a bath. In this case, it may be best to keep hair washing separate from bathtime. If your child associates the two, he may start to fuss about taking baths as well.

The main reason for dislike of hair washing is that babies hate getting water and soap in their eyes, so try to avoid this as far as you can. Specially designed shields are available that fit around the hairline and prevent water and suds from running down your baby's face while you rinse his hair. You may also find that your baby will become less distressed if you hold him in your lap while washing his hair (facing you so that he feels more secure), and use a flannel to wet and rinse his hair rather than pouring water over his head.

Never try to force the issue, and never forcibly hold your baby still while you wash his hair. If hair washing is clearly causing him great distress, give up for two or three weeks before trying again. You can still keep his hair reasonably clean by sponging it with warm water to remove any food or dirt, or brushing it out with a soft, damp brush. The hair will probably become greasy, but this will not do any harm.

CRADLE CAP

Occasionally, you may see red, scaly patches on your baby's scalp. Cradle cap is extremely common and is not caused by poor hygiene or any shampoo you are using. It generally disappears after a few weeks.

Gently washing your newborn baby's scalp every day with a very soft bristle brush and a little baby shampoo in warm water will prevent cradle cap from forming. Even if he has very little hair, brush through it so that scales cannot form.

If cradle cap does appear, smear a little baby oil on his scalp at night to soften and loosen the scales, making them easy to wash away the next morning. Don't be tempted to pick them off with your finger nail: doing so just encourages more scales to form.

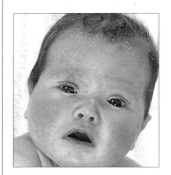

Cradle cap
The scaly patches of cradle cap on a baby's scalp are not harmful, and usually clear up of their own accord after a few weeks. If cradle cap does persist or spread, your doctor may recommend that you use a special treatment shampoo.

BATHING TIPS

Make bathtimes as pleasant and enjoyable as possible so that you and your baby will look forward to them.

• *Before you start, make sure that you have everything that you need to hand.*

• *Always put cold water into the bath first. Test the final temperature with your elbow or the inner side of your wrist.*

• *Keep the water in the bath shallow: about 5–8 centimetres (2–3 inches) is deep enough.*

• *Have your baby undressed for the minimum time: small babies quickly become cold.*

• *Wear a waterproof apron to protect your clothing; a plastic-backed towelling one will feel nicer against your baby's skin.*

• *Put a towel on a radiator to warm, but don't let the towel get too hot.*

• *Use baby bath lotion added to the bath water rather than soap since it is less likely to dry out the natural oils in his skin.*

GIVING A BATH

You can bathe your baby in any room that is warm, has no draughts and has enough space to lay out all the equipment you need. If the bathroom is too cold or draughty, you can fill the baby's bath there or in the kitchen and then carry it to the chosen room (this won't work if it's too heavy).

A small baby can be washed in a plastic baby bath with a non-slip surface, specially designed for the purpose. Place the bath on a large worktop or table of a convenient height (usually about hip height) so that you don't have to bend too much; this will protect your back from unnecessary strain. Some baby baths come with their own stands or are designed to straddle a full-sized bath tub. Either of these will make bathing your baby a far more comfortable task.

GIVING YOUR BABY A BATH

Testing the water temperature
Use your elbow or the inner side of your wrist; the water should be neither very hot nor very cold. A bath thermometer may be a help at first. It should register a temperature of 29.4°C (85°F).

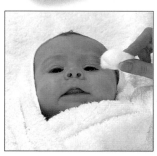

Before the bath
Undress your baby, clean his nappy area (see p. 65), then wrap him in a towel. Clean his face and ears (see p. 54).

Washing his head
Holding your baby as shown above, lean over the bath and wash his head. Rinse his head well and gently pat dry.

Putting him in the bath
Support your baby's shoulders with one hand, tucking your fingers under his armpit, and support his legs or bottom with the other. Keep smiling and talking to him as you place him in the bath.

Washing
Keep one hand beneath his shoulders so his head and his shoulders are out of the water; use your free hand to wash him.

Lifting him out
When your baby is clean and well rinsed, lift him out gently onto the towel, supporting his shoulders and legs or bottom in the same way you did when putting him into the bath.

Drying
Wrap your baby in a towel and dry him very thoroughly. Don't use talcum powder on the nappy area since it could gather in the skin creases and cause irritation.

FEAR OF BATHING

Some babies are terrified of having a bath. Don't force your baby to remain in the water if he's frightened. Try again after a couple of days, using only a little water in the bath. In the meantime, you can give sponge baths (see p. 56) or just top and tail (see p.54).

If your baby continues to be frightened of water, you can try introducing it in a play context. Fill a large bowl and place it in a warm room (not the bathroom). Place a towel next to it, and put some toys into the bowl. Undress your baby and encourage him to play with the toys. If he seems happy doing this, encourage him to splash in the water while you keep a firm grip on him.

After you have done this a couple of times, put a baby bath in place of the bowl and go on letting your baby play. When he tries to get into the water with the toys, you will know he's lost his fear of water. Be patient, however; let him do this once or twice before you wash him in the bath as well as letting him play.

KIDNEY AND
BLADDER
FUNCTION

Once food has been absorbed into the bloodstream, waste is removed from the blood by the kidneys and eliminated from the body as urine.

Urine production Waste chemicals in the blood are removed and dissolved in water by the kidneys. The urine then passes down the ureters and into the bladder.

Voiding Urine is temporarily stored in the bladder, which is emptied through the urethra from time to time. Your baby will not even be aware of passing urine until he is about 15–18 months. The sensation of wanting to pass urine comes several months later, because the infant bladder can hold urine for only a few minutes.

BLADDER AND BOWEL

A newborn baby can need up to ten nappy changes a day. The frequency of changes will decrease, but most babies do not achieve a degree of bladder and bowel control until the second year. Although you can't speed up this process, your help and support will be very important to your child.

PASSING URINE

A young baby's bladder will empty itself automatically and frequently, during both the day and the night. As soon as it contains a little urine, the bladder wall stretches and the emptying action is stimulated. This is entirely normal, and your baby cannot be expected to behave differently, at least until the bladder has developed sufficiently to hold urine for longer periods of time.

BOWEL MOVEMENTS

Once your baby settles into a regular routine, his stools will become firmer and paler (in the 24 hours after delivery, he will have passed a sticky black substance called meconium). You don't need to pay much attention to his stools, and you certainly should never become obsessive or worried about them as long as your baby is content and thriving.

The number of stools a baby passes varies greatly, and initially most bottlefed babies pass a stool for every feed. On the other hand, a breastfed baby may pass only one stool or less a day because there is little waste. The frequency of bowel motions gradually decreases as your baby gets older. It may be that, at the beginning, your baby passes five or six a day, but after three or four weeks he may be having only two movements a day. This is quite normal and should cause you no worry. Similarly, the odd loose, unformed stool or totally green stool is typical of a young baby's bowel movements, and should be no cause for concern unless looseness persists beyond 24 hours. In this case, seek your doctor's advice.

CHANGES IN BOWEL MOVEMENTS

Don't worry if your baby's stools look different from one day to the next. It is quite normal for a stool to turn green or brown when left exposed to the air. If you are worried, consult your midwife or doctor, who will be able to reassure and advise you. As a rule, loose stools are not an indication of an infection. Watery stools, however, if accompanied by a sudden change in the colour, smell or frequency of passing stools, need to be mentioned to your doctor, especially if your baby is "off colour" – pale, listless and off his food.

Blood-streaked stools are never normal. The cause may be quite minor, for instance a tiny crack in the skin around the anus, but you must still consult your doctor. Larger amounts of blood or the appearance of pus or mucus may indicate an intestinal infection, so contact your doctor immediately.

The breastfed baby By the second day, the light yellow stools typical of the breastfed baby will appear. The stools are rarely hard or smelly, and may be no thicker than the consistency of cream soup. Remember that the food you eat will affect your baby, and that anything highly spiced or acidic could upset his digestion.

The bottlefed baby A baby fed on formula has a tendency to more frequent stools that are firmer, browner and more smelly than those of a breastfed baby. They commonly tend to be rather hard. The easiest remedy for this is to give your baby a little cooled, boiled water to drink in between feeds.

WHAT DOES DIARRHOEA MEAN?

Diarrhoea is a sign of irritation of the intestines resulting in loose, frequent and watery stools. In small babies, diarrhoea always has the potential to be dangerous because of the risk of dehydration, which can develop very quickly. Contact your doctor immediately if your baby refuses food or has any of the following symptoms or signs: repeated watery stools; green and smelly stools; a fever of 38°C (100°F) or greater; pus or blood in his stools; listlessness with dark-ringed eyes. If you think your baby is dehydrated, look at his fontanelles. Depressed fontanelles are a definite sign of dehydration; in this case, contact your doctor immediately. Diarrhoea can be quickly cured if it is treated early.

You can start treating your baby immediately yourself if his diarrhoea is mild, and if he has no other symptoms or signs. Continue to nurse your baby if you are breastfeeding; diarrhoea usually clears up well on breast milk, but formula should be made up at half strength, using half the regular amount of formula to the usual amount of water. He may eat only small amounts of food at a time, and will therefore be hungry more often. If diarrhoea is ever accompanied by fever or vomiting, consult your doctor immediately.

BOWEL FUNCTION

In the digestive process, food passes through the stomach into the small intestine and from there into the large intestine. Its waste products are stored in the rectum and then finally eliminated from the body as faeces.

Digestion *All food is broken down in the body by enzymes. Digestion starts in the mouth, where the food is mixed with saliva, and continues in the stomach and the upper part of the small intestine.*

Absorption *Once the food has been reduced to simple molecules, it is absorbed into the bloodstream as it continues its passage through the small intestine. It then passes through the large intestine, where any water is absorbed by the body. The waste products pass on to the rectum as faeces.*

Elimination *Faeces are stored in the rectum and eliminated through the anus. A baby can't control, even for a second, the reflex that causes the rectum to empty. Because the gastrocolic reflex stimulates the rectum to empty every time that food enters the stomach, young babies usually have a bowel movement with each feed.*

GIRLS' NAPPIES

A girl tends to wet the nappy at the centre, or towards the back if she is lying down.

• *Disposable daytime and nighttime nappies are designed differently to take account of where a baby wets the nappy, with the padding at its thickest in the place it is needed most.*

• *You may like to buy frilly or decorative pants to cover fabric nappies: these look pretty under a dress for a special occasion.*

ANATOMY OF A DISPOSABLE NAPPY

Elasticated leakage barriers provide extra protection

Resealable tapes let you check if nappy is clean

Absorbent inner layer has a plastic covering

Efficient leg elastication gives a good fit so there's less chance of leaks

ABOUT NAPPIES

Your first choice in nappies is between disposable and fabric types. Most parents now opt for disposables, but a greater consciousness of environmental issues has led many parents to reconsider the virtues of fabric nappies, which create less waste. Yet the issue is not clear cut: the detergents required to clean fabric nappies can be viewed as pollutants to the water supply, and the energy required to wash them might also be regarded as wasteful. While fabric nappies work out cheaper than disposables in the long run, you need to consider the increased electricity bills for frequent washing-machine runs and the cost in your time. This much is clear: providing that you change the nappy as frequently as is necessary, and that you observe the basic rules of hygiene, your baby will be happy whichever type you choose.

DISPOSABLE NAPPIES

Disposable nappies make nappy changing as simple as it can be. They're easy to put on – no folding, no pins and no plastic pants – and can be discarded when they are wet or dirty. Disposables are convenient when you are travelling, since you need fewer of them and less space to change in; and you don't have to carry home wet, smelly nappies to be washed. You'll need a constant supply, so buy them in large batches once a week to avoid carrying huge loads with your daily shopping. Some shops will deliver nappies.

Never flush disposable nappies down the lavatory as they inevitably get stuck at the S-bend. Instead, put the soiled nappy in a strong plastic bag, making sure the bag is firmly secured at the neck before you throw it out.

FABRIC NAPPIES

Although fabric nappies are initially more expensive than disposables, they work out cheaper in the long run. Fabric nappies involve much more work than disposables because they have to be rinsed, sterilized, washed and dried after use. You'll need a minimum of 24 nappies to ensure that you always have enough clean ones, but the more nappies you can buy the less often you'll have to do the washing. When buying fabric nappies, choose the best quality that you can afford. They'll last longer and so be better value in the long run. Another plus point is that they'll be more absorbent, and therefore more comfortable for your baby.

You can fold towelling nappy squares in several different ways (see p. 65), depending on your baby's size and needs. They are very absorbent (more so than some disposables), so they are good for using at night, even if you have opted for disposables during the day.

Shaped terry nappies are T-shaped, made of a softer, finer towelling than squares, and have a triple-layered central panel for extra absorbency. Their shape means that they are more straightforward to put on, and fit the baby more neatly.

If you are using fabric nappies, you'll need nappy liners to go with them. Choose the "one-way" variety: these let urine pass through but remain dry next to the baby's skin, minimizing the risk of a sore bottom caused by friction or moisture. Liners prevent the nappy itself from becoming badly soiled; they can be lifted out with any faeces and simply flushed away. You will also need at least 12 special nappy pins (these have locking heads to protect your baby's skin) and six pairs of plastic pants to prevent wet or dirty nappies soiling the baby's clothes or bedding.

There is also a type of fabric nappy on the market that offers all the features and convenience of disposables but is machine washable. It is made of several layers of absorbent fabric, shaped to fit, with an anti-leak outer layer, and has secure Velcro closing tabs and elasticated legs.

BOYS' NAPPIES

A boy tends to wet the front of the nappy. Boys' disposables are designed to allow for this, with extra padding towards the front of the nappy.

- *Fold fabric nappies so that more of the fabric is at the front, particularly at night.*

- *Boys often urinate when they are being changed, so cover the penis with several tissues or a spare clean nappy as you take off the soiled one.*

- *Always tuck the penis down when putting on a clean nappy to avoid urine escaping from the top of the nappy.*

FABRIC NAPPIES

PLASTIC PANTS

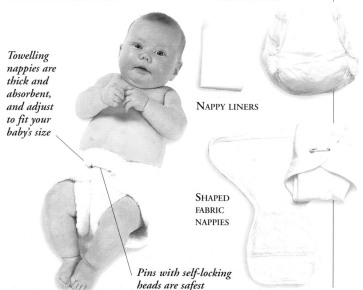

Towelling nappies are thick and absorbent, and adjust to fit your baby's size

NAPPY LINERS

SHAPED FABRIC NAPPIES

Pins with self-locking heads are safest

CLEANING A GIRL

Always wipe your baby girl from front to back (towards the anus), and never clean inside the lips of the vulva.

Remove faeces
Clean off as much faeces as possible with the front of the soiled nappy.

Remove urine
Use a wet cloth or cotton wool to clean the genitals and surrounding skin.

Clean bottom
Lift up her legs as shown, and wipe from front to back. Dry the area thoroughly.

CHANGING A NAPPY

Your baby's nappy will need to be changed whenever it is wet or soiled. How many changes each day will vary from one baby to the next. As a rule, though, you will probably need to change the nappy every morning when your baby wakes, before you put him to bed at night, after a bath and after every feed, including night feeds.

Changing disposables is straightforward, providing you choose the nappy that is most appropriate for your baby's size, so that it fits him neatly and comfortably. With fabric nappies, you can choose the type of fold that suits you and your baby, according to his age and size (see right). You'll need to use liners with fabric nappies, too.

DISPOSABLE NAPPY

Positioning your baby
Lay the nappy out flat, with the tabs at the back. Slide the nappy under your baby so that the top aligns with her waist.

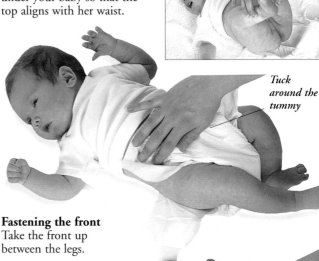

Tuck around the tummy

Fastening the front
Take the front up between the legs.

A comfortable fit
Pull the tabs firmly over the front flap and press to fasten the nappy. It should fit snugly.

FOLDING FABRIC NAPPIES

Triple absorbent fold

This is the most suitable fold for your newborn: its central panel provides good absorbency and it is very small and neat. However, it is not suitable for larger babies. Start with a square nappy folded in four to make a smaller square, with the open edges to the top and right.

Pick up the top layer of the nappy by the right-hand corner.

Pull the corner to the left to form an inverted triangle.

Turn the nappy over so the point is at the top right.

Fold in the middle layers twice to form a thick panel.

Parallel and kite folds

These are for a larger baby. You can adjust the depth of the kite to suit your baby's size. Both start with a nappy laid out in a diamond shape.

Fold the top and bottom points in to overlap a bit at the centre.

Pick up the left-hand point and align it to the top edge; do the same with the right.

Fold the sides in to the centre to form a kite shape.

Fold the point at the top down to the centre. Fold the bottom point up; vary the depth to fit.

FABRIC NAPPY

How to put on a fabric nappy

Slide the nappy under your baby so that its top edge aligns with his waist. Bring the front up between his legs. Hold it in place with one hand while you fold the sides in to the centre. Hold all three layers of the nappy securely with one hand and fasten with a nappy pin.

CLEANING A BOY

Boys often pass urine when released from their nappy. A tissue or clean nappy laid over the penis will minimize mess.

Remove faeces

Clean off any faeces with oil or lotion and cotton wool, using a fresh piece each time you wipe.

Remove urine

Wipe with cotton wool, working from the leg creases in towards the penis. Never try to pull back the foreskin.

Clean bottom

Lift his legs to clean his bottom by holding both ankles as shown. Dry the area thoroughly.

HOW TO MAKE WASHING EASY

Washing nappies will take up quite a lot of time, so use these tips to get organized and simplify your routine.

- *Use plastic tongs or gloves to lift nappies out of the sterilizing bucket; keep them near by.*

- *When changing a nappy at night, keep the dirty nappy in a separate bucket or put it in a plastic bag. Add it to the new sterilizing solution the following morning.*

- *If you use a powder sterilant, always put the water in the bucket first; otherwise you run the risk of inhaling the powder.*

- *Drying nappies on radiators will make the fabric hard and uncomfortable. Use a tumble drier, an outside line or a rack placed over the bath.*

- *You may like to use an air freshener in the nappy bucket.*

Nappy buckets
For sterilization, you'll need two buckets; one for soiled nappies, one for wet ones.

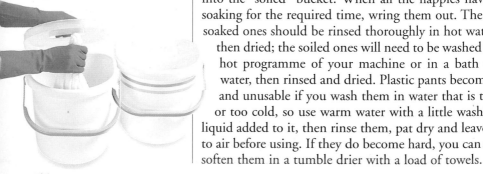

NAPPY HYGIENE

It is very important to wash nappies thoroughly; traces of ammonia will irritate your baby's skin and faecal bacteria could cause infection. Always use pure soap flakes or powders, since strong detergents and biological powders could also irritate his skin. If you like to use fabric conditioner, ignore any manufacturer's instructions and make sure it is completely rinsed away. If you use a sterilizing solution, you will need to wash only soiled nappies, since wet nappies will simply require thorough rinsing. Boiling nappies is not necessary unless they're very stained or have become rather grey; just use hot water for both rinsing and washing. If your baby's clothing gets soiled, don't add it to the sterilizing solution, as the colour will run. Just remove as much of the mess as you can, rinse the garment and wash it as usual.

ESTABLISH A WASHING ROUTINE

Having a washing routine will make life easier, especially if you aim to wash in large loads (to do this, you must have at least 24 nappies). You will need two plastic sterilizing bins with lids and strong handles: one for soiled nappies, the other for wet ones. They should be large enough to hold at least six nappies, with plenty of room for solution, but not so large that you can't carry them when full. You can buy special nappy bins, but any good-sized bucket with a lid will do; bins designed for beer-making are ideal.

Fill the bins with sterilizing solution each morning and always rinse a nappy before putting it in. Rinse wet nappies in cold water, wring out and add to the solution. With soiled nappies, remove as much faeces as possible down the lavatory and hold the nappy under the water spray as you flush it. Squeeze out the excess moisture and put the nappy into the "soiled" bucket. When all the nappies have been soaking for the required time, wring them out. The urine-soaked ones should be rinsed thoroughly in hot water and then dried; the soiled ones will need to be washed on the hot programme of your machine or in a bath of hot water, then rinsed and dried. Plastic pants become hard and unusable if you wash them in water that is too hot or too cold, so use warm water with a little washing-up liquid added to it, then rinse them, pat dry and leave them to air before using. If they do become hard, you can always soften them in a tumble drier with a load of towels.

NAPPY RASH

If urine remains too long in a nappy or on the skin, bacteria from your baby's stools break it down to ammonia. The ammonia then irritates and burns the skin; this is the most common cause of nappy rash. Mild nappy rash (ammonia dermatitis) will appear as small red dots and general redness around the genitals rather than the anus and you will notice a strong smell of ammonia. If it becomes more serious, you will see an inflamed area of broken skin and possibly pus-filled spots. In severe cases, it may lead to ulceration.

Breastfed babies are less prone to nappy rash than babies who are bottlefed. You'll minimize the possibility of nappy rash in any case by following the guidelines given (see right). If your baby does develop a sore bottom, check to see if it is some other rash that might need advice and treatment (see below). If not, go on with your preventive measures (except using barrier cream), as well as the following:

- Change your baby's nappy more often.
- At night (particularly if your baby sleeps through it), use a disposable pad inside a fabric nappy for extra absorbency.
- Once your baby has nappy rash, his skin needs to be aired between nappy changes for, say, 15–20 minutes.

OTHER RASHES IN THE NAPPY AREA

Not all skin conditions occurring in the nappy area are true nappy rash. It's important that you identify a rash correctly so that you can take appropriate action if necessary. Use this checklist to help identify other rashes you may notice in the nappy area; some may need your doctor's advice.

- Heat rash appears as small blisters all over the nappy area in addition to a rash elsewhere on the body. If you are using plastic pants, stop. Leave your baby's nappy off whenever you have the opportunity. Cool your baby down by using fewer layers of clothes and blankets.
- Thrush appears first around the anus as a spotty rash that spreads to the buttocks and inner thighs (you may notice white patches inside your baby's mouth, too). Your doctor will probably prescribe anti-fungal treatments.
- Seborrhoeic dermatitis (very rare in babies) appears as a brownish-red scaly rash on the genitals and in skin creases, especially the groin, and anywhere the skin is greasy, such as the scalp. Your doctor will prescribe an ointment.

PREVENTING NAPPY RASH

The essentials are to keep your baby's skin dry and well aired, and to make sure that nappies are always thoroughly washed and well rinsed.

- *At the first sign of broken skin, start using a nappy rash cream. Creams that include titanium salts are especially effective. Stop using plastic pants, too, as they prevent evaporation of urine.*

- *Broken skin and redness in the leg folds are caused by inadequate drying. Dry your baby meticulously and do not use talcum powder.*

- *Avoid washing your baby's bottom with soap and water since they are both likely to dry out the natural oils in his skin.*

- *Use disposables with a one-way lining or one-way nappy liners with fabric nappies, to keep your baby's skin dry.*

- *Use a fairly thick barrier cream and apply it generously (don't use this with one-way liners or disposables, however; it will clog the one-way fabric).*

- *Thoroughly wash and rinse nappies to make sure all traces of ammonia are removed.*

- *Never leave your baby lying in a wet nappy.*

- *Leave your baby's bottom open to the air whenever you can.*

GIRLS' CLOTHES

FIRST CLOTHES

Unisex stretch suits and romper suits are ideal for everyday wear, but you may prefer more feminine clothes for special occasions.

• *Make sure all clothes are machine washable, since they won't stay clean for long.*

• *Avoid very fluffy or lacy cardigans; fluffy ones will irritate your baby's skin and tiny fingers catch in lacy ones.*

• *A hat can be both practical and pretty. Choose one that has elastic or ties to fasten under the chin and a wide brim for sun protection in summer.*

Everyone loves dressing a baby, and your friends and family will all want to buy clothes for your baby as soon as he is born. You are bound to take great pride in his appearance and might even like to buy some dressy outfits for special occasions, but there's no need to spend a lot of money – he will grow out of his clothes very quickly. Remember that as far as your baby is concerned, anything goes as long as it's soft and comfortable to wear and can be put on and taken off without too much disturbance.

Your baby will posset and dribble on his clothes and there are bound to be accidents and leaks from nappies, so buy only machine-washable, colour-fast clothing and avoid white: it quickly gets dirty and frequent washing makes it look drab.

Look for soft, comfortable clothes with no hard seams or rough stitching. Terry cloth, cotton or pure wool will feel nicer on your baby's skin. Synthetic fibres are soft at first but may become hard and bobbly with repeated washing.

Always choose clothes that are non-flammable and avoid open-weave shawls and cardigans because your baby's fingers could easily get caught in the holes. Check fastenings as well; poppers in the crotch give you easy access to the nappy, and

CHOOSING CLOTHES

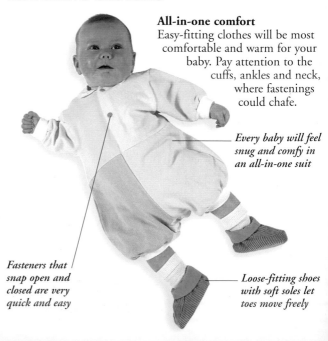

All-in-one comfort
Easy-fitting clothes will be most comfortable and warm for your baby. Pay attention to the cuffs, ankles and neck, where fastenings could chafe.

Every baby will feel snug and comfy in an all-in-one suit

Dressing up
Your little girl will look very special and feel comfortable in a pretty hat and suit with not-too-tight elasticated ankles and cuffs.

Fasteners that snap open and closed are very quick and easy

Loose-fitting shoes with soft soles let toes move freely

BASIC WARDROBE FOR A NEWBORN

6 wide-necked cotton vests or T-shirts
2 pairs socks and padders
1 shawl for swaddling
8 all-in-one stretch suits
2 woollen jackets or cardigans (4 in winter)

2 loose-fitting nightdresses
2 pairs mittens (for winter)
1 padded or fleecy all-in-one pram suit
1 hat with a wide brim and ties or elastic

poppers at the neck mean your baby won't grow out of a garment quickly just because his head is too big for the neck opening. Babies hate having their faces covered, so look for wide envelope necks or clothes with front fastenings. Front-fastening clothes also allow you to dress your baby without having to turn him over. This will make the whole business of dressing more comfortable for him and easier for you.

Note your baby's measurements and take the details with you on shopping trips. Babies of the same age vary greatly in size, so read the height and weight on the label rather than the age. If in doubt, buy the larger size: loose-fitting clothes are warmer and more comfortable than clothes that are too small, and your baby will soon grow into them.

BOYS' CLOTHES

Look for fabrics and designs that are practical as well as smart when choosing clothes for your baby boy.

- *A dungaree and T-shirt set is very comfortable and looks smart. Look out for dungarees that have poppers at the crotch, so you have easy access to your baby's nappy for changing.*

- *Hats with tie-down ear-flaps are cosy in winter.*

- *Don't think tights are just for girls. Babies lose bootees and socks very easily, so tights are practical and warm, even for your little boy.*

- *Tracksuits are extremely comfortable and allow easy access to the nappy.*

- *Strong primary colours look good on both sexes.*

Nightdress
Loose-fitting sleeping garments are comfortable for newborns. A drawstring at the foot end prevents the nightdress from riding up around the body and gives you easy access to the nappy.

Loose-fitting cuffs give your baby plenty of room to move

An envelope neck allows the nightdress to be taken off with greater ease

A drawstring keeps your baby's feet inside and allows for easy nappy changing

Day wear
Soft footwear and a suit with popper fastenings are ideal for a boy and very versatile.

KEEPING YOUR BABY WARM

You may be anxious that your new baby is not warm enough, but a few common-sense precautions will keep him comfortable and safe. Remember that babies can easily become too hot; this could lead to heat rash and is also a factor in cot death.

- *A great deal of body heat is lost through a bare head. Make sure your baby always wears a hat (one with a wide brim and perhaps ear-flaps as well) when you take him outdoors.*

- *Undress very young babies only in a well-heated room and out of draughts, since they cannot conserve body heat.*

- *It's very important to keep your baby's room at a constant temperature. The number of blankets he needs will depend on this temperature (see p. 81).*

- *If your baby is cold, you may need to warm him up. Adding a layer of clothes is not enough in itself; you need to put him in a warmer place first so that he can regain his normal body temperature, or hold him close to share your body heat.*

- *Never leave your baby to sleep in the sun or close to a source of direct heat such as a radiator.*

- *Wrap your baby up if you take him outdoors, but remove outdoor clothes when you bring him inside, otherwise he won't be able to cool down efficiently.*

DRESSING YOUR BABY

At first, you may feel nervous about dressing your baby and trying to support him while putting on and taking off his clothes. Dressing will become easier with practice, so just be gentle and patient until you both get the hang of it.

You need to have both hands free when you're dressing and undressing a young baby, so always use a flat, non-slip surface for this task – a changing mat is ideal. Your baby is very likely to cry as you take off his clothes. This is because young babies hate the feel of air on their naked bodies; they much prefer to feel snug and secure. It's not because you're hurting him, so try not to get flustered by his distress.

PUTTING CLOTHES ON

Putting vest over head
Lay your baby on a flat, non-slip surface; make sure his nappy is clean. Roll the vest up and widen the neck with your thumbs. Put it over the baby's head so that it doesn't touch his face, raising his head slightly as you do so.

Vest sleeves or armholes
Widen the left sleeve or armhole and gently guide your baby's arm through it. Repeat with the other arm. Pull the vest down.

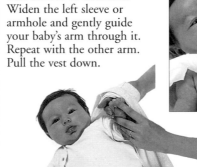

Putting on an all-in-one suit
Lay your baby on top of the open suit. Gather up each sleeve and guide his fists through. Open up each leg and gently guide his feet into the suit. Fasten the suit.

TAKING CLOTHES OFF

Unfastening the suit
Put your baby on a flat, non-slip surface and unfasten the suit. If his nappy needs changing (see pp. 64 and 65), gently pull both legs out of the suit so that his top half stays covered while you change him.

Bend the knee gently as you ease each foot out of the suit

Taking off the suit
Lift up your baby's legs as shown while sliding the suit underneath his bottom and back as far as his shoulders.

Roll the fabric and carefully slide the hand out

Removing the top
Grasp each sleeve by the cuff and gently slide your baby's hand out of it. If he is wearing a vest, roll it up towards the neck and gently pull his arms out of its sleeves or armholes, holding him by each elbow as you do so.

DRESSING ON YOUR LAP

When your baby is three or four months old, he will have developed enough control of his muscles to be able to sit easily on your lap while you take off his clothes. Dealing with his bottom half may be simpler if he's lying flat.

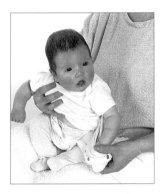

Easy off (and on)
Sit cross-legged so that your baby fits neatly in the hollow of your legs, and cradle him with your arm, since his back will still need some support.

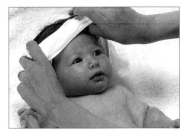

Taking off the vest
Spread the neck wide open with your fingers and thumbs and lift the vest carefully over your baby's head, making sure to keep the fabric clear of his face.

ADDITIONAL CLOTHES

The kind of clothes you buy on top of your baby's basic wardrobe (see p. 69) will be determined largely by your personal taste and how much money you have to spend. There is no single piece of clothing that is essential for your baby, but there are some items that are more practical than others. In summer, for instance, a cotton T-shirt and shorts or a cotton dress are the most suitable clothes because they are cool and leave the baby's limbs free; in winter, a mini pull-on track suit or dungarees worn with a neck-buttoned jumper are good alternatives to an all-in-one stretch suit. As before, stick to clothes in materials that move with your child so that there's no risk of him being uncomfortable, or of the material tearing; terry cloth, cotton and corduroy are ideal. Make sure that his clothes provide easy access to the nappy and that they're machine washable.

Keep an eye on how tight the wrists, legs and neck are on all clothes and buy the next size up if need be. Clothes with poppers at the neck may last longer. Babies often outgrow clothes because their heads can no longer go through the neck opening, but you can just leave poppers undone to accommodate the head. You will probably learn to gauge your baby's size quite accurately, but if you're at all worried, go by the height and weight charts given on the labels, not by age. If your child isn't with you when you're out on a shopping trip, check that the clothes can be exchanged.

As your baby gets older, you may like to dress him in a sleep suit at night as a cosy alternative to an all-in-one stretch suit. If it has plastic soles on the feet, cut a small hole in the middle of each foot to let air circulate so that his feet don't sweat. When the suit gets too short for comfort, cut off the feet for an extra month's wear. A sleeping bag will solve the problem of kicked-off blankets on very cold nights. When buying underwear, choose wide-necked vests that will easily go over your baby's head. Brightly patterned vest and pants sets can double up as pyjamas or T-shirts.

CHAPTER 5

SLEEPING

Unless your newborn is hungry, cold or otherwise
uncomfortable, she'll spend most of the time
between feeds asleep. The amount of time she sleeps
depends on individual physiology, but the average
is about 60 percent of the day. However, don't
expect your baby to sleep all the time and try not to get
worried when she doesn't; some babies are naturally
more wakeful than others right from the start.
As your baby gets older, quite regular sleeping
patterns will emerge. By the time she is three months
old, she will have one main wakeful period a day,
usually at the same time, and this is likely to be
in the late afternoon or early evening.

When planning a nursery, bear in mind that your child will be mobile before long.

• *Make sure that furniture has no sharp edges or corners.*

• *Choose a non-slip floor covering and consider fitting bars and locks to the windows.*

• *Furniture should be stable so your child can't pull it over.*

• *Toys should be stored at floor level so your child doesn't have to stretch to reach them.*

• *Choose wall-mounted lamps to avoid trailing flexes.*

• *Don't overheat the nursery; overheating is a risk factor in cot death (see pp. 81 and 82).*

EQUIPPING THE NURSERY

Your baby may have a room of her own or share yours; once she is sleeping through the night, however, she should have her own space. You'll need little special equipment and you can improvise if need be with household items – a sink will do as well as a baby bath, for instance, and a folded towel doubles up as changing mat – but many parents do delight in the opportunity to equip a nursery.

If this is your first child, ask friends with children which items they have found most useful and then weigh up their advice against your own lifestyle. If there's anything you're unsure about, shop around and have a look through store catalogues before deciding. There will often be many things that you can manage without. The only essentials are somewhere for your baby to sleep, her nappies and clothes (see pp. 62–63 and 68–69) and her feeding equipment.

Don't feel you have to buy everything brand new; look out for secondhand items advertised in local papers or on noticeboards in the local baby clinic. A carrycot will last only a couple of months because babies grow so quickly, so it makes sense to borrow one from friends or relatives if you can. If you buy secondhand items, check for general wear and tear, and make sure that all surfaces are smooth and free of rust for your baby's safety. Check, too, that they still comply with current safety regulations. Beware of painted items; many old-fashioned paints contain lead, which is toxic if ingested (your baby may suck on the side of her crib, for example). Never buy secondhand car seats or harnesses.

BASIC EQUIPMENT FOR YOUR BABY

TRANSPORT	SLEEPING
Carrycot pram (suitable from birth), pushchair or buggy; sling; infant car seat	Carrycot, crib or cot; mattress with waterproof cover; fitted cot sheets; cellular blanket (for newborn); swaddling shawls; baby alarm
BATHING	
Baby bath (with stand); cotton wool; large soft towel; flannel or sponge; baby brush; baby bath lotion; blunt-ended scissors	OTHER
	Bouncing chair; muslin squares

ARRANGING A NURSERY

Once you bring your baby home, you'll be too busy feeding and changing her – and probably too tired as well – to plan your nursery, so do this before she's born.

Try to ensure that the room is as easy as possible to keep clean, with wipable surfaces. Choose furniture without hard edges or corners and make sure that any painted surfaces are non-toxic and lead-free. You'll need plenty of storage space, especially near the changing area; a wide-topped low chest of drawers with shelf space above is ideal, or you may like to build your own. Be sure the top is smooth, washable, and wide enough to accommodate the changing mat. Haircord carpet is the ideal floor covering for the nursery, since it will absorb noise and is warm and hardwearing. If you're worried about keeping carpet clean, vinyl or cork tiles with a non-slip rug or two are a good alternative.

The nursery does not have to be very warm, but it should be at a constant temperature. Around 18°C (65°F) is fine if your baby is covered with a sheet and three blankets; if the room is warmer, she should have fewer blankets (see p. 81). As long as your baby is tucked up snugly, all-night heating will be needed only in very cold weather; a thermostatically controlled room heater is the most suitable.

It is a good idea to fit a dimmer switch so that you can gently bring up the lights without startling your baby. If you like, the light can be left on low as an alternative to a night-light. You may also find a folding screen useful to protect your baby's cot from sunlight and draughts.

DECORATING THE NURSERY

A newborn baby has a very limited range of vision – only 20–25 centimetres (8–10 inches) – but lively colours and decorations will provide a stimulating environment.

• The cheery colours of nature are best. Pastel yellow, blue and grassy green will soothe your baby. Enliven the room with vivid splashes of primary red, yellow, green and blue.

• Hang jolly mobiles above your baby's cot and the nappy changing area. Their colours and movement will make her alert to her surroundings.

• Display bold, interesting pictures in bright colours on the walls and attach fluorescent stars and moons to the ceiling.

• Choose fabrics and wallcoverings that are washable and have lively designs to stimulate your baby.

Mirror made from unbreakable plastic

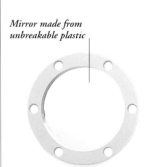

Visual stimulation
Put an unbreakable mirror on the side of your baby's cot so that she can see her own face.

SLEEPING EQUIPMENT

The best choice for your newborn baby is a Moses basket or a carrycot pram; some prams convert to pushchairs for use when she's able to support herself sitting up. Your baby will outgrow baby baskets or cradles quite quickly, so don't splash out on an expensive one unless you're sure you can afford it. When your baby outgrows her crib or carrycot, you'll need a full-sized cot. Choose one with side rails set closely together – 2½–6 centimetres (1–2½ inches) is most suitable – and drop sides so that you can lift your baby out easily. The mattress should fit snugly, so your baby can't get her arm or her leg, or even her head, trapped down the side. The cot will last you until your baby is big enough to clamber out, when you'll need to buy a bed – at about two or two-and-a-half years. The cot mattress should be a foam

Places to sleep
Your newborn baby will be spending much of her time asleep, and she'll be able to sleep just about anywhere. A basket or carrycot is best at first and easily portable, but once she outgrows these, she'll need a cot.

The shade protects your baby from cold draughts and direct sunlight

CARRYCOT

Make sure the cover is washable

MOSES BASKET

Airholes in mattress let your baby breathe if she rolls over on her front

A waterproof cover will keep the rain out

Handles should be near the hood end to take the weight evenly

The gaps between the bars should be in the range of 2½–6 centimetres (1–2½ inches)

The drop side should have safety locks so your child can't let it down

Casters for manoeuvrability and for "rocking"

FULL-SIZED COT

type and have airholes that allow your child to breathe if she turns over onto her front while sleeping. Travel cots are very useful for when you go on holiday or take your baby out with you for the evening. They have fabric sides and are collapsible, so they can easily be carried and stowed.

Because a young baby can't effectively regulate her body temperature, you should always use a cotton sheet with cellular blankets for the cot so you can easily add a blanket or take one away. Once she is a year old, a cot duvet will be suitable. Make sure that any bedding you buy is flameproof and conforms to current safety standards.

Sleeping temperatures Research into cot death has shown that babies who get too hot are at a greater risk of cot death. While the temperature of the nursery is important, the number of blankets is of even greater significance. If the nursery is at 18°C (65°F), then a sheet and three layers of blankets will keep your baby at an ideal temperature. If it is warmer, you should use correspondingly fewer blankets (see p. 81). A lambswool fleece or baby nest is such a good insulator that both carry a risk of overheating, so don't leave your baby in one through the night. Similarly, cot bumpers and pillows can make your baby too hot. Babies lose heat through their heads, so if your baby's head is buried in a pillow or bumper, heat loss will be reduced.

BABY LISTENERS

A baby listener enables you to keep in touch with your baby even when you are in another part of the house.

• *Baby listeners are available in different versions: battery, mains or rechargeable.*

• *With a battery model, look for one that has indicator lights to show if the batteries are low or if the unit is out of range.*

Keeping in touch
Listeners come in two parts: the baby's transmitter and the parents' receiver.

SLEEPING ACCESSORIES FOR YOUR BABY

• Cot duvet (not for babies under 12 months)
• Cotton sheets
• Cotton cellular blanket

• Fleecy blanket
• Tie-on or fitted waterproof sheet to protect the mattress

• Foam mattress with airholes
• Lambswool fleece (not for all-night use)

Young babies are easy to carry, and sleep a lot. This means that they are very portable, so you can still enjoy going out by taking your baby with you.

In the early weeks, it's good for new parents, especially mothers, to get out of the house and be able to relax with friends. This will be easier to do while your baby is young because she will sleep anywhere. A car seat that doubles up as a free-standing chair is ideal for this. It can be safely strapped in place in the car, then carried indoors when you reach your destination while your baby sleeps.

Once your baby starts sleeping through the night, you'll need to stick to a regular bedtime routine, so take advantage of this flexibility while you can.

Sleeping
Ensure your baby is warm and covered but not too warm (see p. 81). A picture of a face on the side of the cot will hold her attention if she's awake.

SLEEP AND WAKEFULNESS

A newborn baby needs a great deal of sleep and unless she is hungry, cold or uncomfortable, it is likely that she will spend at least 60 percent of her time asleep.

Your baby may fall asleep immediately after (and sometimes during) a feed. She will probably pay no attention to noises such as doors shutting or the radio – in fact, she may find droning noises, such as a vacuum cleaner, soothing. Babies' sleeping patterns do vary, though, so if your baby is wakeful after a feed, don't insist that she stays in her cot.

It is important that your baby learns to distinguish day from night. When it grows dark outside, close the curtains and turn the lights very low. Make sure that she is warm and covered and, when she wakes during the night, feed her quickly and quietly without turning the lights up, and don't play with her. In time, she will learn the difference between a feed during the day and one at night.

WHERE SHOULD YOUR BABY SLEEP?

You will probably find it easiest to let your baby sleep in something that makes her portable. During the day, a car seat with a carrying handle is ideal if you drive. If you don't have a car, a carrycot is suitable both day and night since it is easily movable and can be clipped onto a wheeled frame when you go out. When she outgrows a carrycot, she will need a proper full-sized cot (see p. 76).

Sleeping with you At first, some parents will opt to have their newborn baby sleeping with them because night feeds are easier to cope with, and it shouldn't be a difficult habit to break after a couple of weeks. If you do sleep with your baby, let her lie between you and your partner so that she cannot fall out of bed. Don't worry that you will roll on top of her; this won't happen unless you've been drinking or have taken drugs that make you sleep heavily.

Your baby's bedroom Pay great attention to the temperature of your baby's bedroom. Babies cannot regulate their body temperature as well as adults; to maintain the right level of warmth, they need a constant temperature and sufficient blankets to keep them warm, but not too warm (see p. 81). A night-light or dimmer switch means that you can check your baby during the night without waking her.

Sleeping outdoors Except when it's chilly, your baby will sleep quite happily outdoors, but make sure she's wrapped up and visible at all times. Never put her in direct sunlight; either choose a shady area or protect her with a canopy. If it's windy, put the carrycot hood up so it acts as a windbreak. Be sure to put a cat net over the carrycot too.

Clothing Your newborn will need to be changed often, and while she is sleeping she should wear something that gives you easy access to her nappy. The best garment is an all-in-one stretch suit or a nightdress with a drawstring at the foot end so it doesn't ride up her back.

It is important that your baby does not get too hot or too cold. In warm weather, a nappy and a vest will be sufficient. In winter or unseasonally cold weather, you can check that your baby is warm enough by touching the back of her neck with your hand. Her skin should feel about the same temperature as yours. If she feels cold, warm her by holding her close to your body. If she feels too hot and clammy, take a blanket off and let her cool down.

DEALING WITH PROBLEMS

If your baby wakes you frequently during the night or she cries when you try to go back to bed, you'll be short of sleep and you'll then find it difficult to cope during the day. It is essential that you get enough rest, and you should share the responsibility of night feeds with your partner. Even if you are breastfeeding, your partner could bottlefeed your baby on some nights with your expressed milk (see pp. 42–43). Alternatively, get your partner to bring you the baby to feed and then he can change her nappy. If you're exhausted, ask a friend or relative for help, relax your routine, get up late, and take daytime naps whenever you need to.

Encourage your baby to sleep at night by tiring her out in the day with plenty of stimulation: talk to her, pick her up and give her lots of different things to look at. If she wakes up very often during the night because she is wet, use double nappies or nappy liners, and if she cries when you leave her, don't return and pick her up right away. Rocking her cot, removing a blanket or changing her position may be sufficient to soothe her. In the early weeks, wrapping or swaddling your baby (see right) may help her to sleep: the sensation of being tightly enclosed makes babies feel very secure. It is also a useful way to calm a distressed baby.

SETTLING YOUR BABY DOWN

Here are several things you can do to ensure that your baby settles down to sleep.

- *In the first month or so, wrap or swaddle your baby before you put her down. However, do not keep her swaddled all night.*

- *To swaddle your baby, fold a shawl or small blanket into a triangle. Lay your baby on it, aligning her head with the longest edge. Fold one point of the shawl across her and tuck it firmly behind her back; do the same with the other point. Tuck the bottom of the shawl back underneath your baby's feet to keep them covered.*

- *Give your baby a comfort suck from breast or bottle.*

- *Darken the room at night and keep the curtains closed.*

- *In cold weather, place a hot-water bottle in the cot for a short time before you put your baby down, but never leave it with her in the cot.*

- *Hang a musical mobile over the cot to soothe your baby.*

- *If she doesn't seem to be settling down, rock her gently or stroke her back (especially the back of her neck) or limbs to soothe her.*

- *Try carrying her around in a sling and jogging her up and down: your closeness and the sound of your heartbeat will help her to settle down.*

REDUCING THE RISK

By following these guidelines, you will significantly reduce your baby's risk of cot death.

- *Don't smoke, don't allow anyone to smoke in your house and avoid smoky places.*

- *When covering your baby with blankets and bedclothes, allow for room temperature (see chart far right); don't let her get too hot.*

- *Avoid swaddling and tucking in, so your baby can throw off bedclothes if hot.*

- *If you think your baby is unwell, don't hesitate to contact your doctor.*

- *If your baby has a fever, don't increase the wrapping; reduce it so she can lose heat.*

Protecting your baby
The most important thing you can do is put your baby to sleep on her back and be sure she is not too warm.

PREVENTING COT DEATH

Sudden Infant Death Syndrome (SIDS), commonly known as cot death, is the sudden and unexpected death of a baby for no obvious reason. The rate for cot deaths in the UK is 3 per 2,000 live births. In actual figures, this translates to the deaths of 1,134 babies in 1991. Following a campaign to increase public awareness of SIDS, providing parents with the most up-to-date information and useful advice, the death rate was nearly halved to 613 in 1992.

The causes of cot death are still unknown for the most part, and there is therefore no advice that can absolutely guarantee its prevention. There are, however, many ways in which parents can vastly reduce the risk.

SLEEPING POSITION

One of the most crucial risk factors is the position in which you put your baby down to sleep. In most countries, babies have traditionally slept on their backs. In the UK as well, most babies slept on their backs until the 1960s, and the number of recorded cot deaths was low. However, in 1970, special care baby units started the practice of laying preterm babies face down to sleep because it seemed this position improved breathing and reduced vomiting. Eventually, this practice was extended to full-term babies.

In 1965, the significance of sleeping position in relation to SIDS was looked at and debated, but the evidence that had been gathered by this time was not convincing. It was not until 1986, when SIDS rates in different communities were compared, that it became clear that SIDS was a less common occurrence where babies slept on their backs. In the UK by this time, 93 percent of babies were being put in their cots to sleep face downwards.

Quite by luck, when my first son was born in 1972, I avoided this risk by laying him down on his side, thinking that if he wanted to suck his thumb it would be easier for him to do so, and I kept him in this position with small, soft pillows placed in front of and behind him. Since then, research in New Zealand has shown fewer cot deaths in babies placed on their sides, but without support they can roll onto their tummies. The safest position for your baby, therefore, is on his back. Some people will tell you that this position may allow inhalation of posset (regurgitated milk), but there is no evidence to support this.

STRONG EVIDENCE AGAINST SMOKING

There is now no doubt that a mother who smokes during pregnancy increases the risk of SIDS. (She also increases the risk of giving birth prematurely or having a low birth-weight baby.) What's more, the risk increases in proportion to the number of cigarettes smoked. The risk of SIDS in babies born to smokers is twice that for babies born to non-smokers, and the risk increases three times with every ten cigarettes a day. In the region of 365 cot deaths a year could be avoided in the UK if all pregnant women and mothers were just to stop smoking. Studies carried out in the United States now strongly suggest that being exposed to smoke increases a baby's risk of suffering SIDS by 200 percent, and if both parents smoke the risk increases more.

THE IMPORTANCE OF TEMPERATURE

There's also no doubt that overheating a baby from too many nightclothes, too many blankets and too high a room temperature is a contributory factor, as SIDS is much more common in overheated babies. (The risk of overheating alone, however, is less than that from sleeping position and smoking.) Two-thirds of cot deaths occur in winter, when babies may be wrapped up too warmly (continued p. 82).

CONTROLLING THE TEMPERATURE

Keep a thermometer in your baby's room so that you can see how many blankets she needs. At a temperature of 18°C (65°F), a sheet and three blankets are adequate.

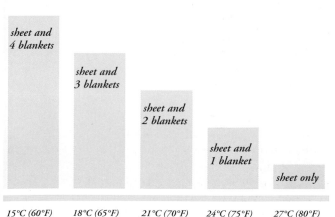

sheet and 4 blankets

sheet and 3 blankets

sheet and 2 blankets

sheet and 1 blanket

sheet only

15°C (60°F)   18°C (65°F)   21°C (70°F)   24°C (75°F)   27°C (80°F)

GETTING HELP

The unexpected death of an infant is bereavement of a particularly painful kind, but support is available to help parents cope with their feelings of bewilderment, grief and guilt (see Useful Addresses, p. 93).

• *Many parents seek help right after the death – sometimes within hours – and telephone support lines are available that can provide information and a sympathetic listener.*

• *In the longer term, parents may seek professional help. The continued support of a health visitor, social worker or religious adviser can be invaluable, so don't be afraid to ask.*

• *Parents may be helped by being able to talk to someone who has been through the same experience, either in support groups or on a one-to-one basis.*

• *Befriending schemes exist in some areas that continue long after professional help may have ceased, and these can be invaluable at times of particular grief such as the anniversaries of the baby's birth and death.*

• *Parents who have lost one baby through cot death are likely to be extremely anxious when another baby is born. Support schemes exist that involve the parents, midwife, doctor and health visitor in making sure the new baby gets the best possible care.*

Many parents increase the amount of bedding when a baby is unwell, but this is not what your baby needs. High body temperature together with infection in babies over ten weeks old greatly increases the risk of cot death. If heat loss is prevented, the body temperature of a restless baby with an infection will rise by at least one degree per hour. A baby loses most heat from its face, chest and abdomen, so lying on the back allows better control of body temperature.

Baby nests, sheepskins, duvets and cot bumpers are all heat insulators, and so should not be used for young babies, because they prevent heat loss. There is no need to heat the nursery all night unless the weather is very cold; just make sure that your baby has enough blankets (see chart p. 81). If you do have a heater in her room, use a thermostatically controlled one that will switch off if the room gets too warm and switch back on again as it cools down.

CONTINUING RESEARCH

Although risk factors have been identified, the causes of cot death are still not close to being understood. Ongoing areas of research include the development of a baby's temperature control mechanisms and respiratory system in the first six months of life, and the discovery that an inherited enzyme deficiency may be responsible for a small number (around 1 percent) of cot deaths. Within the last eight years, a study carried out in the UK connected cot death with flame-retardant chemicals in cot mattresses, but the connection has not been definitely proven.

6

GOING OUT AND ABOUT

Your new baby can go everywhere with you as long as
you are composed and well prepared. It's always worth
spending fifteen or twenty minutes planning how
you are going to get to your destination, what you will
need for the journey, where you are going to feed him
and how you will change him. If you are well organized
and assured, outings with your baby can be a great joy, and
the sooner you start after bringing him home, the better.
Until you feel confident, take someone along to help you.
Having an ally to share the novelty and any problems
will make every trip with your baby more enjoyable.

WALKING AND CARRYING

Your baby will spend most of his time being carried, wheeled or secured in some way, and there is a wide variety of prams and carriers available. Safety and portability should be your main considerations when choosing this equipment.

A sling is by far the most popular way of transporting a newborn: it's light and comfortable, and allows you to carry your baby close while keeping both hands free. Try one on with your baby inside before you buy it, and make sure that it has a good head support for him. A backpack is suitable once your baby can sit up by himself. It has a supportive frame that makes bearing a larger baby's weight easier.

For longer journeys, you will need a pram or pushchair in which your baby can sit or lie down. One in which he can lie flat should be used for the first three months, until he has head control. The pram you choose will depend on your budget and lifestyle. Consider where you will keep it and whether you will need to take it on buses and trains or up and down stairs. Whatever pram you choose, it should have a built-in harness or rings to fix one in place.

Choosing a pram
For the first three months, your baby must be able to lie flat. Reclining pushchairs are available, but a carrycot pram is more versatile and will give longer use. Some models can be converted to pushchairs.

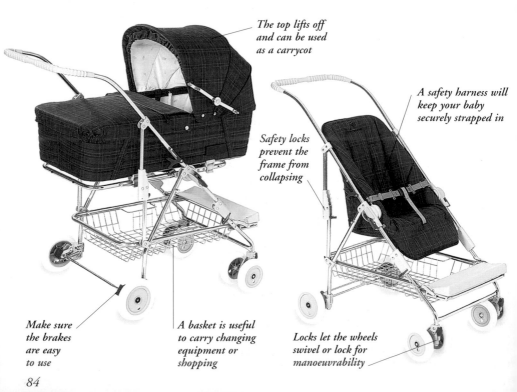

The top lifts off and can be used as a carrycot

A safety harness will keep your baby securely strapped in

Safety locks prevent the frame from collapsing

Make sure the brakes are easy to use

A basket is useful to carry changing equipment or shopping

Locks let the wheels swivel or lock for manoeuvrability

CARRYING YOUR BABY

The sling should have a support to hold your baby's head comfortably

Using a backpack
This is ideal transport once your baby gets too heavy for a sling. Make sure that he is comfortable and that the leg openings don't restrict him.

Using a sling
Your baby will feel safe and secure inside a sling, and it leaves your arms free

Make sure that he is always safely strapped in to prevent him slipping

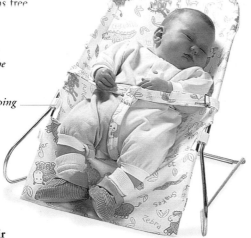

Bouncing chair
When you're out visiting friends with your baby, you can take along a bouncing chair. Your baby can be propped up in the chair so that he can look and see what is happening around him. Always put the chair on the floor, never on a table or worktop.

SAFETY HARNESSES

Your young baby has no fear of falling, so wherever he sits he will have to be strapped in for his own safety.

• *A five-point harness, which has straps for the shoulders as well as the waist and crotch, is the safest kind.*

• *Your baby's pram should have either a built-in harness or fixing points so that you can attach your own.*

• *High chairs often have a built-in crotch strap. They should also have rings to take a safety harness, which you can buy separately.*

• *Many harnesses come with optional reins that you can attach when your baby is old enough to walk.*

WHAT TO TAKE

You'll need basic changing and feeding equipment, and toys to distract your baby.

- *Changing bag or mat.*
- *Fabric or disposable nappies.*
- *Baby wipes.*
- *Nappy cream.*
- *A sealable container or plastic bags for dirty nappies.*
- *A bottle containing a whole feed if you're bottlefeeding.*
- *A change of breast pads if you're breastfeeding.*
- *Hat with a wide brim and ties or elastic under the chin.*
- *Cardigan (not lacy or fluffy).*
- *A couple of favourite toys.*

TRAVEL AND OUTINGS

Time spent planning a trip or regular travel is never wasted. The younger your baby, the more you will have to plan. In the first few months, your baby's feeding schedule may not be very predictable, so you'll need at least one spare bottle if you're not breastfeeding, as well as your usual changing equipment (lightweight bags with portable changing mats are widely available). Plan your route so that you know where you can stop, and where you can change and feed your baby without embarrassment or inconvenience. If you are planning to shop, it is even worth ringing up stores to find out if they have a mother-and-baby changing room, and avoiding those that don't have this convenience.

If your baby is just a few weeks old, it's simply not worth undertaking a very busy outing where you will have to walk a great deal, carry heavy loads, or make lots of changes of transport. Be easy on yourself. Try to take a friend or your partner with you if you can, so there is always an extra pair of hands and someone to help you should you get into a scrape. Your baby can go anywhere with you as long as you are well enough prepared and have something in which to carry him – a sling, pram or car seat.

USING A PUSHCHAIR

If you do not want to carry your baby in a sling, a pushchair is ideal for a small baby, who will fit comfortably and snugly into it. Babies take an interest in their surroundings from a very early age, so as soon as your baby can sit up, angle the pushchair so that he can see what is going on around him.

You must become adept at collapsing and opening the pushchair within a few seconds without any problems, so practise at home before your first outing. If you can't fold up the pushchair efficiently, you will find people jostling to get in front of you when you are in a queue, which will just add to your frustration. At the very least, you should be able to open the pushchair with only one hand, kick it shut with your feet, and know how to operate the brakes – and don't forget that you will have to do all these things while holding your baby. Here are a few safety tips:

- When you open your pushchair, always make sure that it is in the fully extended position with the brakes fully locked.
- Never have your baby in the pushchair without firmly securing him in place with the safety harness.

- Never, ever, leave your baby in a pushchair unattended.
- Should your baby fall asleep in the pushchair, adjust it to the lie-back position so that he can sleep comfortably.
- Don't put shopping on the pushchair handles; it can unbalance the pushchair and your baby may be injured.
- When you stop, always put the brakes on because you could inadvertently take your hands off the pushchair and it might run away.
- Check your pushchair regularly to make sure the brakes and catches work properly and that the wheels are solid.

PUBLIC TRANSPORT

Using public transport can be a real trial, since neither buses nor trains are usually equipped or serviced for mothers and young children. Picture yourself with a pushchair, a heavy, wriggling baby, the baby-changing bag, your handbag, a coat – and possibly a toddler in tow – and public transport becomes the last thing you want to face.

Of course, you can make life easier by never travelling in the rush hour or, with a young baby, carrying him around in a sling. For an older baby, a backpack makes you much more independent, since having your hands free means you can manage everything more easily. Always prepare yourself well ahead of time. I simply would not leave home with my children without some distracting toys, a favourite book, and a favourite snack. All your belongings, including the pushchair, should be collected together prior to leaving and in good enough time so that you can check them over to make sure nothing is forgotten. The same goes for when you are getting off a bus or train: be ready in plenty of time for your stop. Always ask fellow passengers for help.

SPECIAL OUTINGS

Looking after your baby doesn't mean that you can't resume the active and enjoyable life you had before. While he's still tiny, take advantage of his portability and the fact that he will sleep almost anywhere. Dinner in a favourite restaurant or a trip to the cinema will make a welcome diversion in your busy and demanding new routine (but avoid smoky places). Your baby is never too young for an outing, either; indeed, with a young baby you can go just about anywhere and, provided he can look about him, he will enjoy and be stimulated mentally as well as visually by the change of scene, even if he understands little of what's going on.

MANAGING TWO CHILDREN

An outing with just one baby can be a challenge if you are not confident. With a toddler in tow as well, you will need to be especially organized.

- *A double pushchair with sections that are independently adjustable is ideal for children of different ages.*
- *Carry your newborn in a sling, leaving your hands free for your toddler's pushchair.*
- *Four hands are better than two: any trip will be easier with your partner or a friend.*
- *Take a snack, such as fresh fruit, a drink of diluted fruit juice and a favourite book, toy or comforter for your toddler.*
- *Attach toys to the pushchair so you don't have to pick them up again and again.*
- *Avoid having to use public transport or escalators.*
- *Postpone a special outing that you've planned if your toddler is in a bad mood that day, or if you no longer feel like making the trip.*

SHOPPING WITH YOUR BABY

Whenever you take your baby shopping with you, always plan all your movements and stops in detail so that you can use your time most efficiently.

- *Try to fit in a shopping trip between feeds. If you are bottlefeeding and you think the trip is going to be longer than the usual interval between meals, take a bottle containing a whole feed with you.*

- *Always take basic changing equipment in case your child needs a clean nappy. Most big stores have mother-and-baby changing facilities.*

- *For shopping trips by car with a young baby, use a rear-facing car seat, which you can secure in the front or back.*

Harness and reins
Keep your baby safe in his pushchair by firmly securing him with the harness. You'll be able to use the reins and anchor straps when he's older.

SHOPPING TRIPS AND CAR JOURNEYS

Taking a young baby shopping has its own problems. Even if you are going to be out for only an hour or two, he can easily get bored, hungry, fretful and difficult to manage, so it's worth planning ahead quite carefully to minimize stress. Taking a car will make a world of difference: you can feed and change your baby in it, you can load your shopping in the boot and not have to carry cumbersome bags, and you won't have to worry about using public transport.

If you don't own a car, you might borrow a relative's car. If you don't drive, it may be worth asking a friend who does to join your shopping expedition. Try to shop fairly early in the day, when the streets and shops are less busy and there are fewer distractions for your baby. Always try to give your baby a good meal before you leave; that way, you may have two or three hours in which to complete all your purchases without him getting hungry or distressed.

Take whatever equipment you would have with you on any other trip, including feeding and changing equipment. Toys may seem something of a burden, but they will more than pay their way, since you can attach them to the backpack, pushchair or supermarket trolley for your child to play with, and not have to keep on picking them up.

CARRYING YOUR BABY

You need to have your hands free for shopping, and so how you carry your baby is worth some thought and attention. Once your baby is able to sit up with good head and back control, you can put him into your shopping trolley. Many supermarkets now have trolleys with integral baby seats and harnesses, but with the older, tip-up kind of seat, you need to strap your baby in with a harness. A backpack is ideal for carrying your baby on shopping trips: his interest will be continuously engaged, he'll feel very secure with such close physical contact, he should be well behaved and cry very little – and your hands will be free. Since babies are always grasping and reaching for interesting objects, walk down the centre of the supermarket aisles so that he isn't tempted to dislodge tins and packets. Best of all, ask your partner to go shopping with you and get him to carry the baby on his back so that you are free to select and make the purchases.

LONGER JOURNEYS BY CAR

In the cramped circumstances of a long journey, your baby is bound to become fretful. It's your job to make sure that he is cool, fed and changed without fuss and has enough to distract him when he's not sleeping. If the weather is hot, he will become fretful more easily than if it is warm or cool. Never leave your baby alone in a car in hot weather: inside the car, the temperature can rise much higher than the temperature outside, causing him to get quickly overheated and even dehydrated. Always screen your child from bright sunlight by putting a purpose-made blind over the window through which the sun is shining; or attach a canopy to your baby's seat, which will serve the same purpose.

CAR SAFETY

Above all, you need to transport your baby safely in a car. A young baby should go in a rear-facing car seat, which can be used in the front or the back of the car, or in a carrycot in the back seat with proper restraints. If you must travel with your baby held on your knee, always sit in the back. Never sit in the front with an unrestrained baby, because if the car stops suddenly, your baby will be flung out of your arms and will certainly be injured. After any accident, you should replace your seat belts, your child's car seat, and the anchorage kit, since they will have been badly strained and may be damaged. For the same reason, you should never buy secondhand car seats, harnesses or anchorage kits.

FEEDING AND CHANGING

Breastfeeding really comes into its own on a journey, but never feed when the car is moving because your baby would not be safe. If you are bottlefeeding, use disposable bottles and feeds; or make up a batch of feeds, cool them in the refrigerator and then carry them in a coolbag. Alternatively, mix the formula as you need it in a sterilized bottle with boiled water from a Thermos flask. Never try to keep made-up feeds warm; you will only be letting germs multiply.

Take disposable nappies, even if you normally use fabric ones. You can always change your baby on the back seat of the car or on a rug or towel in the boot. You need only top and tail him, but be meticulous about cleaning the nappy area. Always take baby wipes, nappy cream to prevent nappy rash and a sealable container for dirty nappies.

CAR JOURNEY CHECKLIST

As with any kind of outing with your child, the essential thing when travelling by car is to plan and prepare well in advance. The following tips will all help to make things go more smoothly for you.

- *Try to start travelling early in the morning or at night when the roads are empty.*

- *Use a car seat for your baby. Make sure it is correctly fitted and has a safety harness. Keep your baby safely secured in the seat while the car is moving.*

- *If you are travelling by day, carry a window blind to block out bright sunlight.*

- *Have all the feeding and changing equipment you need for the whole journey. Take a sealable container or plastic bags for dirty nappies.*

- *Fill a clean container with cooled, boiled water or take a bottle of still mineral water.*

- *Take a box each of baby wipes and large 3-ply tissues.*

- *Take a rug, baby travelling toys and two or three tapes or CDs with soothing music.*

NOTES

Use this space to record your baby's earliest milestones, for instance, his first smile.

BABY RECORDS

You may think that the exact details of your baby's birth are unforgettable, but you'll find that your memory becomes hazy with time. These birth records and length and weight charts will jog your memory and help you keep track of your baby's progress in his first six months of life.

FIRST BABY

Name ....

Estimated date of delivery ....

Date and time of birth ....

Place ....

Length ....

Weight ....

Blood group ....

Duration of labour ....

Type of delivery ....

Midwife/consultant ....

People present ....

SECOND BABY

Name ....

Estimated date of delivery ....

Date and time of birth ....

Place ....

Length ....

Weight ....

Blood group ....

Duration of labour ....

Type of delivery ....

Midwife/consultant ....

People present ....

GIRL'S LENGTH AND WEIGHT 0–6 MONTHS

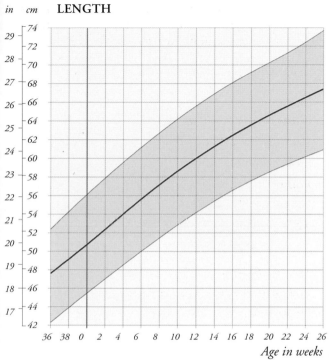

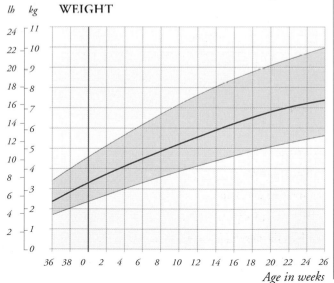

USING THE CHARTS

I believe that no baby needs to be measured and weighed if he's obviously thriving, but we've included these charts for parents who are keen to follow their child's progress.

• *You will probably need to ask your midwife or hospital doctor for your baby's birth-weight and birth-length.*

• *Chart your baby's progress using the measurements taken by your doctor or health visitor, or from readings done at your local baby clinic.*

• *If your baby was preterm, you will need to adjust his age accordingly. For a baby born at 36 weeks, for instance, start recording the measurements at the appropriate point to the left of zero on the charts, and continue to subtract four weeks from his age each time you fill in the charts.*

• *To keep track of your baby's progress with the charts, find his age along the bottom axis and draw a straight line up from it. Now find his length or weight along the vertical axis and draw a line across. Mark a solid dot where the two lines meet. With each week, you'll be able to enter another dot. The emerging row of dots is your baby's growth curve.*

LENGTH AND WEIGHT

When you assess your baby's progress, the most important criteria are his happiness and general well-being. However, you may find it interesting to plot your baby's increasing length and weight on these charts (see also p. 91).

Don't become anxious unless your baby's growth pattern veers away from the centile line (see below). Try not to compare your child to others of his age.

The range of "normal" heights or weights at any given age is very variable. A newborn boy may weigh anything from 2.5 to 4.5 kilograms (5½ to 10 pounds) without giving cause for concern.

Each chart shows the range of lengths or weights into which the majority of children will fall. The darker coloured line in the middle of each coloured band represents the 50th centile, that is: 50 percent of children will fall below the line and 50 percent above it. The outer lines represent extremes beyond which very few children (fewer than 0.5 percent) will fall, but if your child does, consult your doctor.

A child's measurements, plotted regularly, should form a line roughly parallel to the central line. If not, the measurements may not have been correctly plotted or the correct chart may not have been used. Consult your local baby clinic if you feel in any doubt about your baby's progress or well-being.

BOY'S LENGTH AND WEIGHT 0–6 MONTHS

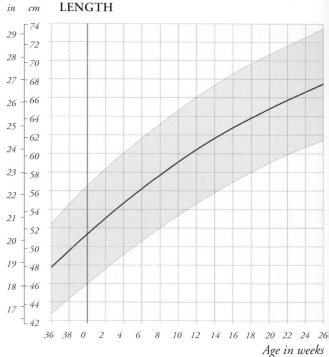

LENGTH

Age in weeks

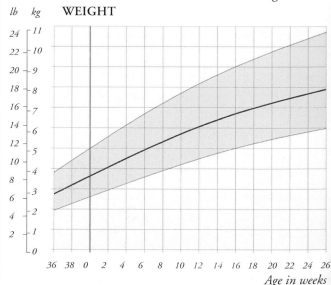

WEIGHT

Age in weeks

USEFUL ADDRESSES

POSTNATAL SUPPORT

Association of Breastfeeding Mothers
PO Box 441
St Albans, Herts AL4 0AS
Tel: 0181 778 4769

Association for Postnatal Illness
25 Jerdan Place
Fulham
London SW6 1BE
Tel: 0171 386 0868

Family Planning Association
2–12 Pentonville Road
London N1 9FP
Tel: 0171 837 5432

Health Visitors Association
50 Southwark Street
London SE1 1UN
Tel: 0171 717 7000

MAMA (Meet-a-Mum Association)
Cornerstone House
14 Willis Road
Croydon CR0 2XX
Tel: 0181 665 0357
For isolated or depressed mothers

National Childbirth Trust
Alexandra House
Oldham Terrace
Acton
London W3 6NH
Tel: 0181 992 8637

PARENTS' GROUPS

BLISS (Baby Life Support Systems)
17–21 Emerald Street
London WC1N 3QL
Tel: 0500 151617 (freephone)
For parents of special care babies

CRY-SIS Support Group
BM Cry-Sis
London WC1N 3XX
Tel: 0171 404 5011
Advice on babies who cry excessively

Foundation for the Study of
Infant Death
14 Halkin Street
London SW1X 7DP
Helpline: 0171 235 1721
Available 24 hours

Multiple Births Foundation
Queen Charlotte and Chelsea
Hospital
Goldhawk Road
London W6 0XG
Tel: 0181 748 4666

National Council for One-Parent
Families
255 Kentish Town Road
London NW5 2LX
Tel: 0171 267 1361

Parentline
Endway House
The Endway
Hadleigh
Essex SS7 2AD
Tel: 01702 554782
Helpline for all ages

TAMBA (Twins and Multiple
Birth Association)
PO Box 30
Little Sutton
South Wirral L66 1TH
Tel: 0151 348 0020
Tamba twin line: 0732 868000

FIRST AID AND SAFETY

British Red Cross
9 Grosvenor Crescent
London SW1X 7EJ
Tel: 0171 235 5454

Child Accident Prevention Trust
18–20 Farringdon Lane
London EC1R 3AU
Tel: 0171 608 3828

Royal Society for the Prevention
of Accidents (RoSPA)
Edgbaston Park
353 Bristol Road
Birmingham B5 7ST
Tel: 0121 748 2000

St. Andrew's Ambulance Association
St. Andrew's House
Milton Street
Cowcaddans
Glasgow G4 0HR
Tel: 0141 332 4031

CHILDREN WITH SPECIAL NEEDS

Association for Spina Bifida and
Hydrocephalus (ASBAH)
Asbah House
42 Park Road
Peterborough PE1 2UQ
Tel: 01733 555988

British Diabetic Association
10 Queen Anne Street
London W1M 0BD
Tel: 0171 323 1531

British Epilepsy Association
Anstey House
40 Hanover Square
Leeds LS3 1BE
Tel: 0113 2439393
Helpline: 0345 089599
Support from local groups

Contact-a-Family
170 Tottenham Court Road
London W1P 0HA
Tel: 0171 383 3555
Supports parents of children with special needs

Cystic Fibrosis Trust
Alexandra House
11 London Road
Bromley
Kent BR1 1BY
Tel: 0181 464 7211

Down's Syndrome Association
155 Mitcham Road
London SW17 9PG
Tel: 0181 682 4001

MENCAP (The Royal Society for
Mentally Handicapped Children
and Adults)
Mencap National Centre
123 Golden Lane
London EC1Y 0RT
Tel: 0171 454 0454
For people with learning disabilities

The Muscular Dystrophy Group of
Great Britain and Northern
Ireland
7–11 Prescott Place
London SW4 6BS
Tel: 0171 720 8055

The National Asthma Campaign
Providence House
Providence Place
London N1 0NT
Tel: 0171 226 2260

National Autistic Society
393 City Road
London EC1V 1NE
Tel: 0171 833 2299

The National Eczema Society
4 Tavistock Place
London WC1H 9RA
Tel: 0171 388 4097

Scope
12 Park Crescent
London W1N 4EQ
Helpline: 0800 626216
Support, assessment and education for people with cerebral palsy

INDEX

A

abscesses, breast, 45
all-in-one suits, 68, 70–71, 79
Apgar scale, 20
au pairs, 24

B

bathing, 54, 56–59
bedding, 77
behaviour, 16–17
birthmarks, 14, 15
bladder, 60
bonding, 10, 11
bottlefeeding, 46–52
    benefits of, 37
    on car journeys, 89
    cleaning bottles and teats, 47
    giving feeds, 49
    hints and tips, 50
    hygiene, 51
    making up feeds, 48
    milk, 46, 48
    routines, 50–51
    sterilizing bottles, 46–47
    supplementary bottles, 43
    warming bottles, 49
bouncing chairs, 85
bowel movements, 15, 60–61
boys:
    behaviour, 19
    clothes, 68
    length and weight, 92
    nappies, 63, 65
    washing, 55
bras, nursing, 39, 44
breastfeeding, 38–45
    advantages, 36–37
    and bowel movements, 61
    on car journeys, 89
    care of breasts, 44
    colostrum, 11, 36, 38, 46
    expressing milk, 42–43
    latching on, 40
    let-down reflex, 38
    milk supply, 38, 39
    positions, 39
    problems, 40–41, 44–45
breathing, 10, 11, 40–41

C

car journeys, 88, 89
car seats, 89
carrycots, 76, 78, 79
carrying babies, 27
childcare, 22–24
circumcision, 55
clothing, 68–72, 79
colic, 31, 33
colostrum, 11, 36, 38, 46
comfort sucking, 41
cot death, 26, 77, 80–82
cots, 76–77
cracked nipples, 45
cradle cap, 54, 57
crying, 11, 18, 30–34

D

death see cot death
dehydration, 61
diarrhoea, 61
digestive system, 61
disposable nappies, 62, 64
dressing babies, 70–71
ducts, blocked, 45
dummies, 32

E

ears, cleaning, 55
engorged breasts, 45
equipment, 74
    bottlefeeding, 46–47
    sleeping equipment, 76–77
expressing milk, 42–43
eyes:
    problems, 12–13
    reflexes, 16
    washing, 55

F

fabric nappies, 62–63, 65
fat babies, 51
fathers, 11
    and bottlefeeding, 37
feeding see bottlefeeding,
    breastfeeding

fontanelles, 12, 21
    dehydration, 61
    washing, 57
foreskin, 55
formula milk, 46
    making up a batch, 48

G

genitals, 21
    appearance, 13
    washing, 54, 55
girls:
    behaviour, 18
    clothes, 68
    length and weight, 91
    nappies, 62, 64
    washing, 54

H

hair:
    appearance, 13
    washing, 54, 57
handling babies, 10, 26–27
harnesses, safety, 85, 88
hats, 70
head, 21
    appearance, 12
    check-ups, 21
    circumference, 14
    handling babies, 27
heat rash, 12, 67
heating, nurseries, 75, 82
hernia, umbilical, 13
hives, 12
hygiene:
    bottlefeeding, 46–47
    nappies, 66

J K L

jaundice, 21
kidneys, 60
lanugo, 13
latching on, breastfeeding, 40
let-down reflex, 38
listeners, 77
love, 10
lungs, 10, 11

ACKNOWLEDGMENTS

Dorling Kindersley would like to thank the following individuals and organizations for their contribution to this book.

PHOTOGRAPHY
All photographs by Jules Selmes except Ron Sutherland/Science Photo Library, page 13 (right)

ILLUSTRATION
Aziz Khan

MEDICAL CONSULTANTS
Dr. Margaret Lawson, Dr. Frances Williams

ADVICE AND ASSISTANCE
Child Growth Foundation (length and weight charts), National Childbirth Trust,
The Vegetarian Society

EQUIPMENT
Boots the Chemist, Children's World, Debenham's, Freeman's Mail Order

ADDITIONAL EDITORIAL AND DESIGN ASSISTANCE
Nicky Adamson, Caroline Greene, Maureen Rissik, Ruth Tomkins

INDEX
Hilary Bird

TEXT FILM
The Brightside Partnership, London